HEAR WHAT THE SPIRIT SAYS TO THE CHURCHES

Edited by Gerhard Linn

HEAR WHAT THE SPIRIT SAYS TO THE CHURCHES

Towards Missionary Congregations in Europe

MISSION SERIES

WCC Publications, Geneva

Cover design: Edwin Hassink

Cover photo: Gordon Gray – Resurrection window in the
Presbyterian church in Lisburn, Northern Ireland (see p. 55)

ISBN 2-8254-1142-6

© 1994 WCC Publications, World Council of Churches,
150 route de Ferney, 1211 Geneva 2, Switzerland

No. 2 in the WCC Mission Series

Printed in Switzerland

Contents

Introduction

This is a book of the congregation, written by and from local congregations to other local Christian communities in the hope that many of them might be encouraged by the reports published here to take their own initiatives of responding to what God's Spirit is saying to them.

In early 1989 the Conference of European Churches and the mission section of the World Council of Churches initiated a long-term process of promoting "missionary congregations in a secularized Europe". Unlike earlier similar efforts it was intended to be carried from the very beginning by local congregations in different countries. There were no methodological models for conducting an international ecumenical study in a way that it would be done by real local congregations rather than by experts drafting recommendations for congregations. A guide for a self- and situation-analysis by local Christian communities was drafted and then tested in some congregations. Published in English in *International Review of Mission* (Jan. 1992, pp.109-18), this guide is also available in Czech, French and German. Originally it was meant to provide a framework of necessary steps and crucial questions to enable congregations to compare their own methods and results with those of other congregations involved in a similar effort. Yet it soon became obvious that this impulse offered for local adaptation was widely misunderstood as a recipe, "the Geneva model" for congregational renewal. So we have decided not to include it in this book.

There is no recipe for the renewal and transformation of congregations for mission. There are theological criteria to help orient those who want to learn and to move. But what is decisive is the motivation of at least a group of members in a congregation: their common wish and will to find out what God's agenda is in their place, in order to respond to it with imagination shaped by love, to discover it through prayer, analysis and listening anew to the word of God. Thus we promoted this ecumenical process for missionary congregations in Europe by identifying local Christian communities which are seeking to respond authentically and specifically to the challenges God has prompted them to see — in other words, congregations which are trying to hear what the Spirit is saying to them.

Ecumenical gatherings were arranged for groups delegated by such congregations to exchange experiences and offer mutual advice. The largest of these was the All-European Ecumenical Gathering of Congregational Groups in July 1993, in Potsdam, Germany; and its "Letter to Congregations" is printed as an appendix to this book.

Some of the reports that follow were presented at Potsdam; others were prepared for other gatherings; and a few were commissioned especially for this book. The result is of course far from complete. Many countries are missing; and none of the numerous interesting examples of renewal in European Roman Catholic parishes is included. Some aspects of congregational renewal are missing, in particular, examples of efforts — for instance in parish seminars — to communicate the essentials of Christian faith to adult people who are seeking orientation.

The examples from congregations are organized under seven themes (though it is clear that some of the reports could have been located under more than one rubric). Each of the seven chapters is opened with a page of biblical quotations and introductory phrases and questions that might help readers to apply the reports to their own congregations.

Before the congregational reports are two essays offering a general framework for defining what witness and what service are needed in Europe today. The first develops theological perspectives, the second socio-political changes in Europe and their implications. The combination of the two underlines the need for the encounter between situation and biblical message as a means for knowing God's agenda in concrete terms.

Following the examples from congregations are some voices from other continents. The first two were written as a reaction to the reports from European congregations; the third is a shortened version of the keynote address in Potsdam by Professor Kosuke Koyama. The final essay is by a Swedish local pastor, who tells how one congregation was inspired by examples from other congregations to initiate its own open-ended learning process, whose result is not yet known.

I should like to thank all who have contributed to this collection — including those whose papers could not appear here. Special thanks are due to the members of the international editorial group: Donald Elliott, London, Olga Ganaba, Moscow, Anders Roos, Sollentuna, Sweden, and Dietrich Werner, Hamburg. They invested much time and energy in reading and editing reports and in searching for additional ones to cover other aspects. It has been a great joy to work with them.

GERHARD LINN

1. Theological Perspectives on Congregational Renewal

Dietrich Werner

The crucial importance of local congregations in the missionary and ecumenical renewal of the church was recognized by the third assembly of the World Council of Churches (New Delhi 1961):

> The place where the development of the common life in Christ is most clearly tested is the local situation, where believers live and work. There the achievements and frustrations are most deeply felt. But there too the challenge is most often avoided. It is where we live and work together daily that our Lord's own test is most clearly imposed, "by this shall all men know that ye are my disciples, if ye have love one to another" (Section III, 19).

Amidst rapid secularization, individualism and the spread of Western consumerism throughout Europe, the future credibility of the Christian churches and their power to attract people will depend crucially on the ecumenical openness and missionary impact of the different forms of local congregation (parish, spontaneous extraparochial membership, house church, action group). Missionary presence is not so much a matter of programmes, institutional strategies or public declarations as of Christian life-style in communities that radiate hope and solidarity. Since the momentum of mission is basically sustained by local congregations, the churches in Europe need to give priority to them — and to questions relating to their renewal. While the ecumenical study on "Structures for Missionary Congregations" in the 1960s drew attention to the relevance of a globally oriented view of mission for the renewal of the local congregation, a fresh awareness of the urgency of local missionary and ecumenical renewal has emerged since the end of the 1980s, both in the extended study on "Missionary Congregations in a Secularized Europe" by the Conference of European Churches (CEC) and in the work of the WCC programme on Education for Mission.

Dietrich Werner is director of studies at the Mission Academy in Hamburg, Germany.

Challenges in a new situation

Four principal reasons underlie this learning process:

1. Since the political changes in Central and Eastern Europe, the churches there have been facing fundamental upheavals and huge challenges to renewed witness. At the same time, new interest in religious tradition and Christian faith has placed growing demands on them, and many are being obliged to rediscover or strengthen their diakonia and catechesis. Conversely, many Western European churches and congregations confront the challenge of fostering new vitality and depth in their worship and spirituality. CEC's call to churches and missionary societies "to unite in making mission emphases a priority in all their work for the rest of the century, and declaring their commitment to common witness and shared participation in God's mission" ("Letter from Crete", 1991) indicates a growing need for East-West exchanges between congregations and churches in Europe in order to learn from one another in missionary practice.

2. Declining attendance at services in many churches in Western and Northern Europe means that "missionary renewal" is often interpreted primarily as increasing the number of members and attendance at services. The underlying intention of ecumenical and missionary congregational renewal, however, is a commitment to a holistic concept of mission which focuses on promise, avoiding an image of the church and a missionary strategy that focus on what is lacking. To make one's church's own interests the yardstick and motivation for action is to miss the opportunity for possible renewal in mission. What matters is discovering the promises God has given to those who gather together locally in his name and transcending social, cultural and mental obstacles to communicating God's love to all people, to the local *oikoumene*. A congregation which begins to do what the Spirit of God reveals to it as it seeks renewal will perhaps also find that God is making it grow.

3. The social, ethnic and cultural changes in many parts of Europe have far-reaching implications. Migration, the development of religious pluralism, the growing gap between rich and poor, the increasing influence of the new religious movements — all pose a challenge to congregations. The pace of change often outstrips their capacity to cope with new situations. Developing relevant plans for missionary renewal requires a clear grasp of the changes in the local and regional context. Where the structure of the congregation or the mode of its proclamation sets it apart from its changed social and cultural context, a new effort to create awareness of its environment — a switch of perspective from itself to

others — is needed. The goal of the learning process for ecumenical missionary renewal of congregations is a new inculturation of the Christian faith in post-Christian Europe which speaks to people of this day and age while being bold enough to keep a critical distance from Western consumerism.

4. The greater possibilities for contact with churches in Eastern Europe, the presence of ecumenical workers and missionaries from overseas in Europe (for instance, the Swedish project "Mission to the North"), the increasing number of Christian congregations of non-European origin in Western Europe and the movement towards direct partnerships between congregations in Europe and overseas have created many more opportunities for encounter between Christians in different contexts. Such exchanges and the mutual strengthening and support they provide are an important motivating force in the learning process for ecumenical missionary renewal. No congregation should be left to struggle alone on the arduous road of new experiments and changes for missionary renewal. Ecumenical partnerships can be an important source of encouragement towards missionary renewal. The emergence of a European network of ecumenical congregational partnerships, involving congregations which maintain relations overseas (North-South partnerships) and with Orthodox or Protestant diaspora churches in Eastern Europe (East-West partnerships), could be a significant factor in promoting ecumenical renewal of the churches in Europe.

The congregation from the standpoint of *missio Dei*

1. *The congregation as a sign of missio Dei.* The congregation's responsibility for mission has its roots in God's promise to create a new heaven and a new earth in which love, peace and justice will prevail (Psalm 85:7-13). Missionary renewal of the congregation therefore means sharing, in all aspects and forms of congregational life, in the process of God's mission, which aims to achieve *shalom* for the entire creation. Even in a minority situation, church and congregation exist not for themselves, but so that in and through them something of the fullness of life God has promised for everyone may become perceptible. The congregation's mission thus lives by the prayer "your kingdom come". Where it is imbued with the spirituality of this hope it will open up to the people around it and become a living sign of a society that cuts across boundaries.

Promotion of congregational life from an ecumenical perspective serves God's mission, the realization of God's healing purpose for the whole of his creation. To be a congregation means to live out the presence of God and declare it, to be present in God's name in places where life is destroyed, endangered or impaired. Consequently, in the congregation people must feel that the love of God reaches to them and that they have been invited to take part in the incarnation of this love for others. The awakening of faith, the deepening of fellowship, the discovery of different gifts and the enabling for service are common elements of a single learning process which makes missionary presence possible. The congregations portrayed in the main body of this book are all expressions of such participation in the living movement of God's mission.

2. *Mission as crossing boundaries and sharing life*. The principle of mission is to cross boundaries and to experience solidarity, meeting with the stranger and with others in the spirit of Jesus. In this the first priority is not crossing geographical frontiers, but transcending the social, cultural and economic frontiers which separate people from each other (and often from the life of the congregation) even when they live close to one another. God's promise aims at an inclusive community of "all in each place". When a congregation matures into a community in which life with its everyday cares is really shared, its missionary impact grows. Spiritual and social renewal of the congregation often go hand in hand.

What the congregation proclaims should correspond to its outward appearance. External ecumenical openness and partnership should be matched by internal ecumenical openness and inclusiveness. For congregations in present-day Europe, the development of a life-style that embodies hospitality towards strangers is a central task for evangelism. A congregation which is simply concerned with itself and has given up outreach to others cannot be missionary any more than one which is unaware of or ignores the real boundaries, divisions and barriers in its own social surroundings.

3. *Mission as conversion: the integration of the missionary and conciliar processes*. The missionary renewal of faith and the conciliar process for justice, peace and the integrity of creation belong together like the two foci of an ellipse, for both have to do with conversion to the faith, with enabling people to turn to the one Lord of life. Conversion to God's *shalom* — the complete changing, *metanoia*, of our attitudes and life-styles — concerns what is ultimately important for us, our society and the world. Congregations should be places where we enquire into the ultimate values of our life and of society. In the midst of a marked trend towards a life-style determined by competition, consumerism and individualism, congregations should develop an alternative way of life that makes it

possible to discern something of God's vision for this world. Faith is always personal, but never private. Evangelism and social involvement, spirituality and socio-political diakonia and responsibility for the world are therefore not contradictions but essential complementary elements in the renewal of the congregation.

Ecumenical congregational renewal is thus directed towards the integration of evangelism and social action, of the "ecumenism of faith" and the "ecumenism of justice". The prophetic dimension (responsibility in relation to the world) and the saving and faith-awakening dimension of a congregation (diakonia, pastoral care and worship) must not drift apart. A congregation can be a "resisting congregation", committing itself in society against the threat to life and the destruction of life, only if it is a "supportive congregation", in which stability and the capacity to bear burdens can come into existence through fellowship and common prayer.

4. *Mission as taking sides: the congregation as advocate and source of hope for those in society who are weak and cannot speak for themselves.* Growing social tensions and a widening gap between rich and poor even in Western Europe mean that the tasks and approaches of "mission in solidarity with the poor" or "missionary presence with the poor", often considered a concern exclusively for the churches in the South, are becoming a central task of the churches in Europe. Mission in Christ's way means going along with him in his approach to the poor and deprived and being changed in the process. Frequently a congregation is changed only when it has itself undergone a radical conversion through encountering the reality in which the weak and oppressed live. For the church today it is not so much a question of speaking out for the deprived as of becoming a place where the victims of unemployment, competition and the pressure to do well can find their own voice. Where the language of everyday suffering and social protest has disappeared from Sunday worship, it must surely open itself afresh to the viewpoints of those marginalized in our society.

Ecumenical congregational renewal can be seen as a practical attempt to become the church in solidarity with the poor within a wealthy country. This will be possible only if the congregation is felt to be a place where the deprived feel they are recognized and have human dignity, and discover afresh their own possibilities for acting responsibly on their own initiative.

5. *Mission and dialogue: the four areas of congregational ecumenicity.* Ecumenism in the congregation is frequently regarded only as local interconfessional cooperation and cooperation with partners and churches

overseas. Our starting point, however, should be a wider picture of the ecumenical dimensions of a congregation. Dialogue and cooperation with people of other religious convictions are also part of a congregation's ecumenical character and missionary impact. A congregation which understands its mission in ecumenical terms will develop its missionary presence in four areas:

• *Local church ecumenism*: the fellowship of all Christians in each place. No congregation can meaningfully promote congregational life on its own or against other congregations. "Every church acting in mission is acting on behalf of the whole body of Christ" (WCC seventh assembly, Section III, B.1).

• *Social ecumenism*: reaching out across boundaries towards other social classes, deprived groups and the marginalized in its own society and in the church.

• *Interfaith ecumenism*: witness, dialogue and common life with those of other worldviews, religions and cultures in its own immediate vicinity or in the region.

• *Global ecumenism*: the perspective of the one world, shared responsibility for issues relating to the survival of humanity and fellowship with the ecumenical Christian world.

The relation between these dimensions should be balanced. The internal and the external ecumenicity of a congregation must be in step with each other, for the fundamental aim of missionary renewal is that the *whole* gospel should find living expression for the *whole* human being through the *whole* church in the shape of the local congregation.

6. *Mission as sharing in the Holy Spirit: the communication of charisms*. To be capable of mission, congregations need a new experience and certainty of the gifts of the Spirit already at work in their midst. The missionary competence of a congregation is not primarily a matter of external structure, organization and programme, but concerns its entire social and spiritual life-style and the possibility of experiencing the presence of God within it. Where people experience the Spirit of God they become free from themselves and for others: they are encouraged to use their own gifts. The missionary renewal of the congregation therefore has very much to do with a new spirituality in worship and with a participatory congregational life. Among their members — including "nominal" ones — many congregations have considerably more spiritual gifts and talents at their disposal than are actually put to use. In many places public worship is spiritually impoverished, as is evident in a lack of spontaneity, devotion, joy and sense of fellowship. The Canberra

assembly called on the churches "to rediscover the New Testament teaching that each Christian has at least one gift of the Holy Spirit for the building up of the church" (Section III, D, Recommendations).

Ecumenical renewal of the congregation can draw on experiences of charismatic renewal to give a greater place to active expectation of the working of the Holy Spirit in blessings, intercessions and prayers for healing during worship. Of course, it must guard against spiritual elitism or separatism and avoid treating the reality of the Spirit of God as dependent on the *extra*ordinary manifestations (speaking with tongues, ecstasy, healing) of the Spirit.

7. *Mission as transformation: working together on a sustainable counter-culture.* Missionary renewal in Europe at the close of the twentieth century is faced with a variety of signs of a crisis in Western civilization. Secular society is not a sphere devoid of religion; rather, "principalities and powers" (materialism, selfishness, the mania for growth, racism, individualism, lack of consideration for the environment) are at work in it, posing a serious threat to life in different societies. A missionary congregation which focuses on God's promise to preserve the integrity of the whole creation and renew it will have to become the precursor of a viable counter-culture. Missionary congregations can become the sponsors of a culture of nonviolence within a nationalist and xenophobic society. They can become oases of humanity and mutual esteem in the midst of apathy. They can become places where people have time for each other and for God amidst the hustle and bustle of an urban life-style that leaves no time for the fountain of life. They can become a refuge of hope in the midst of anxiety over the future and the gloomy outlook for the coming generation. If congregations are to work together to develop a sustainable counter-culture which by its structure does less violence to nature and the relations between men and women, and which is less energy-consuming, less isolating and less disruptive of solidarity, then we need people who have experienced the forces of healing and hope in their own lives.

2. Hints and Guesses: Changes in Europe as a Challenge to Congregations

Alastair Hulbert

... you are the music
While the music lasts. These are only hints and guesses,
Hints followed by guesses; and the rest
Is prayer, observance, discipline, thought and action.
The hint half guessed, the gift half understood, is Incarnation
    (T.S. Eliot, *Four Quartets: The Dry Salvages*, 1941, Part V).

We are in effect at a crossroads in the history of Europe... Even if on the surface of the sea nothing is yet visible, deep down the currents are beginning to change direction... (European Commission President Jacques Delors to the churches, 1992).

For decades, Europe has dragged the rest of the world into deadly conflicts. Today there is hope that it can radiate — as a unifying entity — the spirit of peaceful cooperation (Vaclav Havel, *Summer Meditations*, 1992).

Alain Minc, author of *Le Nouveau Moyen-Age*, claims that the collapse of communism was the greatest shock the world has experienced since the fall of the Roman empire. And Cardinal Martini of Milan has recently declared, "There are no landmarks given from outside any more as in the time of communism. It is inside the self that the work has to be done..., for we are living in a sort of whirlwind..."

We are in the middle of a mutation from an energy-based society into an information-based society. Information and control technologies are not the same as such technologies of the energy-based era as mechanical and chemical engineering; they yield more goods and services with less human labour. The mechanization of the economy has gradually substituted machines for people. Full employment is a thing of the past.

The world of images is also going through a revolution, the consequences of which are far from being completely grasped. According to

Alastair Hulbert from Scotland is secretary of the European Ecumenical Commission for Church and Society in Brussels, Belgium.

Le Monde Diplomatique (Aug. 1993), it is "a revolution comparable to the appearance of the alphabet, the birth of the printing press, or the invention of photography". Space probes are reportedly so near to discovering the origins of creation that they are described as "peering into the face of God".

The "panic sower" of the millennialist imagination of a thousand years ago is out again scattering his seed. As the millennium draws to an end it is hardly surprising that apocalypse is in the air. But it carries messages of anticipation, expectancy, annunciation as well. In the words of Edgar Morin, "the new European awareness is awareness that everything is uncertain, that the threats themselves are threatened, and that, as the poet Hölderlin said, with danger salvation is also at hand" (*Penser l'Europe*, 1989).

It seems that only superlatives are adequate to describe the new reality and history of this continent and, indeed, the world. As if all-powerful Zeus, disguised as a snow-white bull, had visited the Mediterranean shore once more to rape fair Europe — and all the terror and hope which that myth spoke to the classical consciousness has returned.

* * *

After the explosion of enthusiasm that greeted the reunification of Europe at the end of the 1980s, two developments in particular darken the future and contribute to Europe's present sense of demoralization: the nationalist wars in Eastern Europe and widespread unemployment. They incite horror and despair. No resolution is in sight, though the prevention of war was the original reason for establishing the European Community and the creation of new jobs was what the Single European Market promised for ordinary citizens. A senior official in European Union foreign affairs recently admitted to a church delegation in Brussels that he did not know what was to be done, adding significantly that "there is no guarantee that the market system will survive".

The collapse of communism and the subsequent bewilderment of the capitalist market economy have left the world like a boat in troubled waters. The polarization of the cold war masked the fact that on both sides of the old divide lived the same species of *homo viator* (Man, the traveller, with a historical purpose), the same children of the Enlightenment and the industrial revolution, the same believers in history and progress. Nobody seriously questioned the materialist consumer societies of either side while they were wreaking their quiet destruction on nature and culture. Politicians had more pressing preoccupations. Now the arrow of progress is broken. Progress is no longer able to deliver the goods, and the consequences of that are slowly dawning. Without a credible historical purpose to replace discredited ideologies, without the drive and direction of the race towards "development", the whirlpool of nationalism, economic recession and environmental disaster put the whole continent at risk. Yet the leaders of Europe and the world continue to believe in progress and development. The crisis of the economy as analyzed in "Growth, Competitiveness and Employment", the European Commission's White Paper of December 1993, evokes not so much "changes in Europe" as a response of "better management, greater efficiency, no change".

Why when the Commission publishes Green Papers (consultative documents) on European social policy, audiovisual policy and so on, is there a White Paper (a definitive policy document) only on European economic policy? The answer is clear: there can be *no alternative* to the economic paradigm as it exists. The model is not up for discussion. The crucial challenge facing civilization in Europe today is not so much the change the continent is undergoing as its refusal to contemplate change.

The English dramatist Howard Barker's play "The Europeans" recalls a Europe pervaded like today's by turmoil and disaster. Set in the aftermath of the liberation of Vienna from the Turks in 1683, it was written just before the outbreak of the current barbarous wars in the Balkans. The character of Katrin, a Viennese citizen who has been raped and mutilated by Turkish soldiers, reminds us of the women in Bosnia, Croatia and Serbia who have been victims of atrocity three centuries later. In the terrible final scene Starhemberg, an imperial general who has taken Katrin into his protection, is preparing to give away her bastard child to the Turkish commander. "Oh, the great chaos of this continent...," he cries. "How do we escape from history? We reproduce its mayhem in our lives..."

Is this the destiny of Europe? How do we escape from progress and from civil war, from meaninglessness and the void? Is there no way out? Does God have nothing else in store?

* * *

"The Europeans" is subtitled "Struggles to Love". God has inside experience of the life we live because Jesus lived it. That makes a difference. In spite of appearances to the contrary, especially at a time of transition such as now, we believe history has a meaning and purpose. It is not ultimately negative. And this faith touches our ordinary lives and affects how the communities of which we are members respond to change.

Mark 4 describes Jesus teaching a large crowd beside the Sea of Galilee. He spoke to them in parables about witness and service — the sower, the lamp, the mustard seed — which nobody could understand. The story concentrates on the disciples, and how Jesus explains his meaning to them. The chapter ends with Jesus and his friends crossing over to the other side of the lake. This is the group he gathered as the core of the Jesus movement. It is night and the sea is stormy.

In telling this story Mark was sending a message to small Christian communities, struggling to live their faith under the persecution of the Roman empire, battered by power-oriented politics, suffering the brutal domination of a foreign ideology. Mark puts it in such a way as to bring it close to home. He speaks about men at sea, a handful of frightened sailors in a storm who are afraid for their fishing boat, their livelihood, their families, their very lives. Jesus is in the stern of the boat, asleep in the midst of the chaos. Panic-stricken, his disciples wake him, "Master, do you not care if we perish?" He rebukes the wind. The calm takes them by surprise. "Why are you afraid? Have you no faith?", he asks. They are filled with amazement. He is in control in a way they never imagined, greater and grander than nature. His reassurance is at the same time troublesome and challenging.

* * *

It was a hopeful sign that 1992, the 500th anniversary of the voyage of Christopher Columbus to the Americas, brought a significant reversal of judgment and perspective on the half-millennium since 1492. A strong swell of opposition among native Americans and critical voices on the other side of the Atlantic led to widespread repudiation of the triumphalist celebration of European expansion and the domination of Latin America.

Local Christian communities certainly played a part in that change of heart, though the same could not be said without nuance of church hierarchies. The Roman Catholic Church did not seize the opportunity to confess its responsibility for the expulsion of Jews and Muslims from Europe in 1492. Despite all the hype in Seville, Madrid and Barcelona, the Spanish church made no effort to rehabilitate St James, patron saint of Spain and the conquistadors and of so many acts of barbarism in the new world. That might have put the churches in a stronger position to oppose the ethnic cleansing of the 1990s.

But there are other tasks to be done in setting straight the record of Europe's Christian past and in freeing ourselves for convincing action in the present. It is important to see our actions, small and seemingly insignificant though they may be, in the context of deeper movements for change within society. Three powerful undercurrents are feminism, culture and nature. They relate closely to the ecumenical definition of justice, peace and the integrity of creation. What follows are some "hints and guesses" about witness and service in these areas.

If it is true that the churches today are in the throes of an ecumenical "winter", it is perhaps most evident in the shifting dynamics among women and men in church and society. The feminism of twenty to thirty years ago, with its commitment to ordinary women, its exuberance and anger, its sense of humour and exposure of the absurdities of male dominance, may have been eclipsed for the time being; but the fullness and freedom of feminine and masculine nature and social expression remain as vital a challenge as ever for both men and women. Society at large is still radically divided about the place of women. The institutional church is no exception, as demonstrated by the ecclesiastical musical chairs being played in England over the ordination of women. So much remains to be done. We must not cede the initiative to institutional players, for it is in the intimate context of grassroots groups that alternatives for the community of women and men can best be imagined, created and experienced.

The secularism of modern European culture is deceptive, disguising a rigid credo in the garb of liberal materialism, as if knowledge properly applied in the search for "a better life" were everything: no need for God. Science, technology and economics are the Old Testament, New Testament and systematic theology of the age. The culturally sanctioned dogma of modernism is everywhere. The presumption (not far from the truth) is that everyone, including "churchgoers", believes it. In such a context, the task of Christians in base communities, house churches and Bible study groups is perhaps to promote the equivalent of the "atheism" for which the early church was persecuted — "atheism" in the sense of refusal to accept or believe in the dominant ideology or religion. What is required is a form of confessing church, which sets itself apart with a clear "Here I stand!"

The difficulty lies in discerning the true nature of the culture we inhabit. Developing a theology of resistance to its all-pervading influence requires breaking new ground. Inspired by the prophetic vision of the Bible, Christians must join forces with others outside the church to open up new fields of social discourse as Western civilization advances deeper and deeper into a cul-de-sac. The old political categories of left and right are no longer determinative: conservative and socialist policies differ less and less. Nor is the "green" critique enough: transnational companies and governments alike have co-opted environmental issues. A third dimension of public choice is necessary, one which highlights sufficiency, self-motivated activity and human well-being over against consumption and accumulation, employment and the race for development.

But such talk must not remain at the level of theory. The laity has a wide choice of movements to join which seek to elaborate this alternative approach in practice: *Transport 2000* in the UK, which is looking at alternatives to the motor car; *Europe '99: Projet de Civilisation* in France, with its counter to the European Union White Paper on "Growth, Competitiveness and Employment"; *Basic Income* groups in many countries, with their proposal of an allowance for every man, woman and child as a starting point for an alternative way of tackling unemployment; *local exchange trading systems*; and so on. None would pretend to be comprehensive — all the more reason for Christians to be involved. The parables of the lamp, the leaven and the salt all point to the challenge of Christian commitment in affairs of the world. If worship, prayer and Bible reading were what they might be, Christians would surely be a much more critical force than they are.

Speaking in Glasgow in 1990 philosopher and theologian Raimundo Panikkar warned: "I believe it will take a catastrophe much greater than Chernobyl or Ethiopia, one from which our civilization may not recover, for us to be brought to our senses." The juggernaut of Western culture has a seemingly infinite capacity to absorb and co-opt opposition. In the wake of the UN Conference on Environment and Development in Rio, the environmental critique of development is being neutralized by its incorporation into the very object of its censure. Both left and right on the political spectrum increasingly take "sustainable development" to mean "sustainable growth", though this is an impossibility in a finite world. The human-caused catastrophes of recent years have largely been ignored, just as Pharaoh discounted the plagues of Egypt. Such catastrophes are a dramatic indication of the need for change, but instead there is a hardening of heart among the rich and powerful. If Christian community is a place where that can be understood, could it not also nurture learning and prophecy based upon its awareness of the dangers? Are we using our capacity to disbelieve the secular faith of European modernism? Who else but "atheists" like us might denounce the folly of our age? Should Christian community not be the place par excellence where common sense is rehabilitated, where the know-how and competence of ordinary people are reclaimed from the monopoly of professionals who disempower them and hinder the reorientation of society? And this includes first and foremost the clergy as a professional class.

* * *

New forms of mission are required to confront this situation. Such a vocation was described by the WCC seventh assembly:

> There is an urgent need today for a new type of mission, not into foreign lands but into "foreign" structures. By this term we mean economic, social and political structures which do not at all conform to Christian moral standards (Section I, para. 46).

This vision of the missionary vocation should be systematically elaborated alongside the much more commonly recognized call for mission to individuals and communities. What is required in this time of institutional demoralization and social unease is a closer association between ecumenical missionary bodies responding to this need and local Christian communities. How can we invent new forms of cooperation both at the level of ecumenical organizations and at the grassroots?

In the wake of the collapse of communism and the consequent uncertainty, there seems to be a greater openness to discussing issues of mutual concern among politicians and civil servants at the European level. In Brussels and Strasbourg the churches are developing a "theology of insistence" vis-à-vis the European institutions. It constitutes an ongoing missionary programme: advocacy on issues of justice and ethics and critical dialogue about the economic and cultural paradigm. The term "theology of insistence" was used by Marshall Fernando of Sri Lanka during an ecumenical visit to the European institutions in Brussels in October 1992; he distinguished it from a "theology of resistance". But the term need not be limited to dialogue with state or inter-governmental institutions. It is particularly relevant to industrial mission and any other field where Christian faith and understanding lead to missionary insistence about the meaning and direction of society (consumer groups, environmental lobbies, media alternatives, parent-teacher meetings, etc.). The witness and service of local Christian communities must cooperate with mission to structures in various forms. But where are the ecumenical conferences dealing with mission in this broad sense? From where does the theological inspiration come to elaborate a strategy?

* * *

What is this tangled search for a way into the future, this pursuit of the truth in a time of transition, this yearning for life lived freely and contagiously, if not the "hint half guessed" that comes from the experience of faith in Jesus Christ? The movement of God towards us in love and vulnerability draws us out of ourselves towards God. All the changes in Europe cannot engineer that transfiguration. The Enlightenment, which still flows sluggishly in our veins, knows no equivalent purpose or progress. No scientific or technological solution can answer the riddle of the "gift half understood", the love of God that made it possible. Only in this mystery may we hope to discover the meaning of our lives; only through the inexplicable may we perceive the course and direction of the world.

The why and wherefore of the church is to celebrate this mystery, to keep alive such hints and guesses. The challenge of change, however heroic the response it may evoke in Europe or elsewhere, is not in itself enough to indicate what has to be done. In the person of Jesus Christ lies the clue to our witness and service. Janet Morley puts it this way in a collect for Advent in *All Desires Known*:

> God our Deliverer,
> whose approaching birth
> still shakes the foundations of our world,
> may we so wait for your coming
> with eagerness and hope
> that we embrace without terror
> the labour pangs of the new age,
> through Jesus Christ. Amen.

In the midst of the tumult and chaos of Europe, Christian mission to individuals and to structures and ideologies cannot do without the strength and encouragement that come from life together based on the life and death of Jesus. Christians must give themselves the space and time to weave webs of mutual support and to think and act responsibly together. This involves constantly rediscovering the art of celebration, renewing liturgy and rooting our faith in the search for meaning.

In the base group to which I belong, the agenda roams the landscape of social and cultural change, searching for ways ahead. But that is not enough. An indispensable part of our time together as friends is also the *ceilidh* or party where, besides food and drink, each one contributes song or dance, poem or playing an instrument for the enjoyment of all.

3. Responding to Social Change

No one sews a piece of unshrunk cloth on an old cloak, for the patch pulls away from the cloak, and a worse tear is made. Neither is new wine put into old wineskins; otherwise, the skins burst, and the wine is spilled, and the skins are destroyed; but new wine is put into fresh wineskins, and so both are preserved (Matt. 9:16-17).

How do we discern the voice of God's Spirit?

Changes in the society at large or in a congregation itself may be challenges through which the Spirit speaks to a Christian community. A congregation may get new neighbours, altering the social composition of the neighbourhood. Or political changes may give the congregation the chance to play a new role. How does a congregation respond to such a challenge?

It may be that the changes are not that obvious, but a congregation nevertheless feels that it has to change in order to be faithful to God's call. Then a deliberate effort to understand the situation may help to discern the voice of God's Spirit.

When you look back over the last ten years of your congregation's life:

- What changes do you see?
- How did your congregation respond to these changes?
- How should your congregation respond to them?

BERLIN-KREUZBERG, GERMANY

The Thomas Church and its Neighbourhood

Uwe Dittmer

In the 19th century, the Thomas Church in the Kreuzberg district of Berlin is said to have been the largest congregation in the world, with some 150,000 members. Today about half the population of the district is foreign migrants, and the membership of the congregation is around 3400.

The Thomas Church congregation was directly affected by the building of the Berlin Wall in 1961. In the years that followed, many new buildings were put up in the district, but because they were so close to the border between the German Democratic Republic and West Berlin, they were allocated only to reliable members of the party or the state apparatus. The western part of the parish included an exceptionally large church building which stood right next to the wall and was very little used. Efforts are now being made to use this building with others as a community church and cultural centre.

The district of Kreuzberg has the highest concentration of foreigners in Berlin, above all Turkish migrant workers brought to the city as a labour force since the 1960s. Today it is perhaps the unsafest area of Berlin. It is the quarter with the highest number of young people living in squats, and there have been violent clashes between different groups and the police. The Christian communities here face tasks that are unknown elsewhere in Berlin.

In this setting the now much-reduced Thomas Church congregation lives alongside others. Of its 3400 registered members, between 20 and 40 attend Sunday worship, six to eight form the choir, eight to twelve are interested in a Bible discussion group. There is a nursery school and two youth groups, one for foreign and one for German young people. The Thomas Church has two pastors and six paid church workers. In the same parish there is a Roman Catholic congregation, St Michael's.

To a far greater extent than in many other places, the Thomas Church plays an important role in the life of the neighbourhood. This was not really of its own choosing. In recent years when disputes and clashes have arisen between squatters and the city authorities, the church has acted as an intermediary. When one house was forcibly evacuated, it offered the occupants, who had nowhere else to go, shelter in its premises. The congregation has also become increasingly aware of the problems of foreigners living in Germany, and today it enjoys the confidence of the people in this area, who in turn are less hesitant about coming into the church.

In cooperation with the Catholic congregation, the Café Krause is open every day for homeless people, who receive a free breakfast. Each Wednesday a group of women plans — at their own expense — something special as a treat for the destitute. Sixty to eighty people come. In the winter months the city authorities give the café a financial subsidy; during the rest of the year the two congregations bear the financial costs of running it.

Because about half the children in the nursery school are Turkish, "Christian education" has to be played down and the staff refrain from engaging in mission. Care is taken to choose subjects and texts which are equally accessible and appropriate for Muslims and Christians. The community life in the nursery school helps the children to experience and learn about other religious rites and customs. Christian children join in celebrations of Turkish Muslim festivals; Muslim children do the same for Christian festivals.

Besides the nursery school, there is also an open programme of work with schoolchildren in which boys and girls of both faiths as well as those with no religious affiliation take part. Once a month church workers and mothers prepare a service for mothers and their children — Christian, Muslim and non-religious.

When an effort was made to form a joint youth group for foreign and German young people in the church, it turned out that the same German young people who attended school with foreign classmates as a matter of course refused to be together in their free time and stopped coming. Recently, therefore, there has been only a youth group for foreigners in the congregation. Strictly speaking this is not a Christian youth group; the important thing is to listen to them, to learn about them, to look for opportunities for talking with them, to play and to answer their questions. The congregation plans to make a new attempt to form a group of German young people, hoping that when it has become established the two groups can be brought together occasionally and venture on another attempt at common activities.

Between the eastern and western parts of the parish lies a strip of land which until 1989 formed the border and no-man's land. Here homeless people have settled in old cars, caravans and circus wagons. Through negotiations it was possible to persuade the district authorities not to drive them off and — for the time being, at least — to preserve this space for them to live in and even to improve it by connecting it to electricity supplies and providing disposal services. As a result, people from the "camp" have come to the parish and even attended worship. Unlike the others who come, they are not freshly showered, neatly dressed, with middle-class manners. Many have problems with alcohol and other drugs. Gradually, the congregation is learning what it is like when people "from the highways and hedges" come into the church and upset the normal order of things. And when a group stays on after the service to discuss the sermon and one or two people from the caravans join them, the discussion is likely to be livelier than is customary in a traditional Christian congregation. But the congregation knows that this should actually be normal in the church and, despite the inconveniences, they consciously accept it.

Cooperation with the Catholic congregation also extends to spiritual life. Once a month a group from the Catholic church comes to the Bible discussion group and often attends the Protestant church service as well. A group of Jesuits living in the area also occasionally joins in the Bible study and worship. For the Protestant congregation these encounters are a challenge to think about the forms of its own spiritual life, to adopt new ideas in its fellowship and to learn from others.

But there are also many non-Christians who do not come to the church services or to the Bible discussion group. These include the people from "over there" — the eastern part of the district "on the other side of the wall". There are many unemployed among them, intelligent people who are just waiting to be able to do something worthwhile. The pastors had the idea of forming a citizens' association, which anyone can join without necessarily becoming officially linked with the congregation. But the association needs a room, and the congregation provides it. It needs people with experience, and the two pastors can help. The citizens' association plans to monitor municipal services, future building and urban planning in this part of the city. One of the two pastors is in fact a well-known expert in town planning. In this way, contacts come about, people get to know and talk to one another, perhaps even reach mutual understanding and sometimes — quite incidentally — have conversations of a quite different kind.

In terms of numbers, the Thomas Church is inconspicuous in the huge city of Berlin, even in comparison with other congregations. But in terms of its understanding of the mission of God and its part in it, this congregation offers an example of what can be done when a small group of people really enters into the life of the neighbourhood.

OSTSTEINBEK, GERMANY
Ecumenical Renewal of the Local Congregation
Jürgen Wisch

Oststeinbek and Havighorst, on the eastern fringe of Hamburg, were small villages which grew into sizeable communities after the second world war through the influx of refugees and the development of new housing estates. These newcomers brought their own traditions and their own gifts into the parish. From 1958 to 1987 one pastor ministered there; and, in the typical style of the national church, Sunday services, baptisms, marriages, burials and confirmations were the main activities of the congregation.

The pastor represented "the church" in many aspects of the village life. Indeed, until about 1970 the Oststeinbek civil community and the parish church district were not completely separate entities. The church was present in the life of the villages in the person of the pastor and in the performance of its public duties, while local community leaders were also likely to be members of the church council.

As Hamburg and the new suburbs grew, this pattern changed. Many detached dwellings and some smaller blocks of rented accommodation were built. The growing population meant growing church membership, but at the same time the sociological structure of the population changed, becoming more urban-oriented. The life of the people was more clearly divided between home and work (90 percent of the adult working population commutes to Hamburg, mostly by private transport; locally there is only a primary and an intermediate school).

Following the retirement of the pastor in 1987, there was a fresh start in activities with two young pastors, a second pastoral post having been created because of the growth in population. In 1991 the pastors turned with interest to the idea of redefining the identity of the local congregation in its situation of change through an "Ecumenical Renewal of the Local Congregation" (ERLC) project. Paving the way for this was an outreach project using holiday leisure activities. For a week a team of volunteers from the congregation organized family worship, bedtime stories, evening services, public discussions and many other events in a tent on the marketplace, thus directly reaching local people who had little or no contact with the church. Through events such as an evening called "The Church Pub" and a football match, social contacts were also formed — something which had been quite uncommon in the recent past. The experience of this week, which had highlighted the boundaries between the parish and the community and at the same time helped to open them up, was the decisive factor in making us take up the suggestions from Geneva for the ERLC.

To begin, the pastors and the deaconess visited several people in the congregation, representing different sections and areas of life in Oststeinbek, who might be interested in the project. A support group of nine persons met together with two advisors (who had introduced the congregation to the idea of the ERLC).

At the first meeting hopes and suggestions were exchanged:

• clarify the identity of the congregation: what do we as a congregation want to be and why;

• find an acceptable course between our distinctive profile as the community of Jesus Christ and cooperation with associations, parties, etc.;

• seek forms of congregational life which make it evident, in accordance with Matthew 11:3ff., that Jesus is alive and present in the daily life of Oststeinbek.

It became clear that the members of the working group had very different pictures of what they considered the church congregation to be. During the second evening, group members therefore spent the time in reading aloud to one another biblical passages that they found important for understanding the congregation.

At the suggestion of the support group, a weekend retreat took place in the parish hall in March 1992. Church workers and members of the parish council tried to form a clearer picture of the congregation, taking account of the ideal and the reality. The two outside advisors were also involved in the preparation and running of this weekend.

To begin, the participants were asked to put themselves in the place of a neighbour or someone in public life who had no church connections and to act that role for the others. Typical examples were:

— A man and his wife had left the church because they found it difficult to keep up the mortgage payments on their new house and pay church taxes at the same time. The man was indignant when the pastor then had reservations about baptizing their baby. "That's what the church is for, after all."

— A man complained that his wife was always going to church and spent all her time doing church work without getting anything for it. "What does she get out of it? I can't understand it!"

— A woman from the local district council had realized that things were being done in the congregation in the social and political field. She wondered if there might be an opportunity for more cooperation but she wasn't sure the people in the church would want that.

This role play produced a lively picture of how "outsiders" see the congregation — what they find strange about it and what they expect of it.

Another exercise invited participants to present the congregation in the form of a "landscape". Materials were provided (brushes and paints, clay, building bricks, natural objects) and plenty of time allowed. At the end, we read Isaiah 35, which uses many features of the landscape to symbolize the coming of the Messiah and salvation. This produced three different and highly imaginative pictures. While the work was going on there were lively conversations about the ideal and the reality of congregations and about what constitutes the centre of church life — worship or fellowship in the various groups.

As we looked at the many and varied symbols and images different people chose for the congregation, we noted that they nevertheless came together to form a whole. As someone put it, the congregation has an "inner oikoumene". On that basis, the Sunday service of public worship was prepared in three groups, with each of the three pictures being presented in the church. This was well received by the congregation who found it very lively.

In discussing these pictures, we identified three poles which form a field of tension within which the church community may be understood:

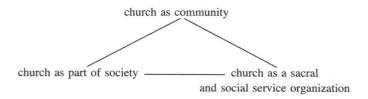

church as community

church as part of society ————————— church as a sacral
and social service organization

Each of these three poles determines the shape of the congregation, but they differ in importance. Until the 1970s, the Oststeinbek congregation had been largely determined by the two latter poles. The church was then still seen as a social institution and part of the village's distinctive identity. With increasing changes in society, in the patterns of people's daily life and in the church's understanding of itself, the first pole has become more important in the congregation's life and conception of itself. Above all it has become a place of fellowship and the centre of a variety of group activities.

Two further tasks, also in the framework of ERLC, were thus identified:

1. To establish where and how the congregation can and should carry out its share of responsibility to local society in the district, including cooperation with other groups and institutions.

2. To analyze how the expectations of the church as a service organization relate to or conflict with the high expectations of the church as a place of fellowship and participation — first of all through discussion with the people who hold such expectations.

In subsequent meetings further thought was given to the different kinds of ties and relations people have with the church. The idea of making home visits in the parish (including to people who had left the church) and re-examining our own "insiders'" image of the church was suggested. It became clear that very different expectations of the church were represented even within the support group itself. We became aware of how much effort was required to create *one* congregation from people who have such different spiritualities and ideas of the goal.

Some members of the support group were afraid others might be offended if they honestly said what they thought. Others felt we were being too slow in drawing the practical consequences. People did realize that this group was a kind of model of the congregation itself, and that its own experience in dealing with these limits could be useful for everybody. But in the long run they did not have the energy and willingness to get involved in this process, and so in early 1993 the group decided to call it a day. One reason for this was certainly the long intervals (on the average, two months) between the meetings, which meant that the work suffered from a lack of continuity. Nevertheless, the results of the work continue to be felt in the congregation in the form of a wider and more open view of the local community and the expectations of those who have no church connection.

ST GEORG, HAMBURG, GERMANY

Mission in the City

Kay Kraack

Hamburg has two "saintly" districts, each near one of the city's main arrival points: St Pauli at the port and St Georg at the main railway station.

The former is renowned far and wide as a red-light district, but the latter is scarcely less notorious. Almost everything can be bought here — bodies, drugs, gambling, entertainment. Besides being Hamburg's second red-light district after St Pauli, St Georg is also widely known as a centre of drug-peddling and an unlovely dumping ground for asylum-seekers, the homeless and problem families. Yet it is also home to a few long-standing residents who have been joined more recently by many younger people with wide-ranging cultural and intellectual interests.

The major shift in the social structure of St Georg was brought about in the 1960s by the planned demolition and renovation of the district at a time when the trend was for many people to move to the outskirts of the city. Except for a few families, the once-prosperous middle-class heart of the district moved away. Socially vulnerable groups, above all migrant families, took their place. Today the proportion of foreigners living here is around thirty to forty percent.

These developments had considerable repercussions for the tradition- ally minded church congregation (founded in the twelfth century). The loss of its middle-class membership base brought lowered income and radical cutbacks, among other things, in staff. The massive drop in membership was reflected in constantly falling attendance at worship and a general loss of status in the district. The growing feeling of being a dwindling minority led to widespread apathy or nostalgia. Successive and unsettling changes of ministers (first three, then two permanent posts) was one result. The congregation's traditional profile no longer corre- sponded to the needs and it lost its cohesiveness as a community. Increasingly, the individual areas of work (ministry, children's day-care centre, old people's home and nursing home, work with the elderly, church music, youth work) took on a separate existence and pursued their own interests. The parish council, largely made up of members living outside the area, took care of the financial administration but did little to set priorities in the actual work.

In the mid-1980s, some rethinking of the work of the congregation took place, partly because of another change of ministers. Two main ideas dictated the line for the future:

1. *Taking the district seriously as our parish.* The congregation cannot continue to see itself in terms of its great middle-class past but must look to the future, taking seriously the district as it now is, with its new composition and new inhabitants and new concerns. Moral authority is no longer automatically conferred on the congregation and its workers by their office; they must now earn respect by doing competent work relevant to the needs of the district.

2. *Working with others.* In a district like St Georg, with pluralistic values and advanced secularization, church work can hope to succeed only if it is carried out over a long period by a staff who can work together as a team and agree on the basic principles. Individuals operating alone in separate areas of work are bound to fail because of rivalries within the congregation and an overload of work.

Putting the ideas into practice

1. By starting a professionally staffed youth work department, the congregation opened up to the new reality of the district and began to adapt to its altered social structure. On the basis of this it sought links with other bodies engaged in social and educational work in the district and with the authorities. To facilitate joint work it set up a "Social and Educational Initiative", bringing together various institutions, initiatives and groups — schools, day-care centres, counselling services, political parties, local authorities, churches. This evolved into a generally recognized platform for neighbourhood work across political lines, and the pastors played an important role in promoting cooperation and communication. As this initiative gradually won recognition and became more popular, a range of networks and links was formed. Cooperation and relevance to the needs of the neighbourhood became the new watchword of the congregation and the district.

During this period of about six years the congregation became a generally accepted partner. Its facilities and experience (communication skills, administration, finance) were of basic importance for the work. Initial hesitations about the church in general gave way to acceptance of its special expertise in social and neighbourhood issues. One important reason for this was certainly that the church and its representatives were not overbearing. Acting simply as one institution among others, they contributed to the work in a strictly practical way. Religious themes were not raised as such, although they were often brought in by others in personal conversations ("Oh, you're a pastor! I thought you were a social worker...").

On the basis of the relationships and recognition developed during this period, we have once again been putting more emphasis on religious-philosophical themes over the past two years. Building on the credibility earned in the field of social work, we now have tried to arouse interest in the religious dimension of our identity as well. The congregation set about building a "second bridge" of religious-cultural events — readings and music by local artists, concerts with suppers, an Easter night celebration with meditation, worship, a café and a disco — to complement its activities in social work, diakonia and local politics. These were of a high standard, open-minded, ranging from serious to light-hearted and entertaining, not claiming to know all the answers. They have been well-received, attracting especially people between 25 and 40 who are often otherwise critical of or even hostile to the church, though the more traditionally minded older nucleus of the congregation also enjoys them.

In short, the congregation has regained a firm and accepted place in the life of the local community and is seen as a unity with all its different areas of work. It is a generally recognized and appreciated partner because it is cooperative in its approach but nevertheless firmly partisan in its commitment to the local area. Its members have become correspondingly more confident and have shaken off their apathy.

2. As the work of a congregation is all too often beset by rivalries, divisions and cliques, it is tremendously important to create and maintain a general atmosphere of openness and solidarity.

At first, the desired links between the different areas of work took place only through the ministers, who regularly attended the working meetings of the different departments and tried to promote an exchange of ideas and coordinate efforts. The sense of a new collective identity in the congregation as a whole was slow to develop. It also took a long time to establish a relationship of openness and trust between the church workers and the ministers. Mutual resentments, not least along employer-employee lines, were difficult to overcome. Here the parish council was helpful as the body where discussions could take place and decisions be made. Representatives from the different areas of work were always present; free access to information and transparency in all decisions were emphasized. Important decisions were taken only by consensus.

Staff planning required particular care. In the often time-consuming process of recruiting staff or ending someone's appointment, what we considered in particular, besides specialized competence, was ability to work as part of a team and willingness to adapt to the needs of the district. We were looking for highly qualified people. In return the congregation offered a good working climate and specialist support, as well as the highest possible salary for the job. The importance of this latter aspect is often treated too lightly in church circles.

Stages of the process
1. The change of direction in the planning of the work came in the first instance from the ministers. Following yet another change of staff, the two colleagues who found themselves working together were both by training and personality interested in such a change. The joint planning and organizing of many events (worship services, communicants classes, discussions with church workers, etc.) took up a great deal of time. In addition, approximately one full day per week was devoted to reflection on the work and relations in the team of ministers. It was not always easy to put all one's cards on the table, but this was essential to guard against any kind of rivalry and enable us to see the respective personal roles and differences as an enrichment and an opportunity.

The large amount of the ministers' time taken up by networking, management and communication obviously meant that time had to be saved on other things. For instance, it proved impossible to continue having a minister present at every one of the different congregational activities, as had come to be expected. In the areas which had traditionally received a large amount of attention (the elderly and adults), this reduction was initially misunderstood as a downgrading of their importance, but over time the shift in focus of pastoral activity came to be accepted. The ministers now provide back-up and support for the voluntary leaders of the different groups rather than planning the actual work.

The aim was to make these areas of work — hitherto very dependent on the ministers — largely independent, without of course losing contact with them. But if that is to happen, it is important that the pastors are available to help with their expertise and *time* whenever they are really needed.

Usually pastors have their preferences. The viability of the process described here depends on how far the congregation as a whole can be brought to accept it as a permanent change in their style of relationships. Only when the leading bodies and groups have understood how the new style works and come to appreciate it will they be able to maintain this approach for the future and make it a criterion in selecting any future ministers.

2. The understanding of a congregation described here, based on communication and networking, implies some important ecclesiological aspects. *Within the congregation* it calls for a considerable reduction of hierarchy in relationships and leadership structures. All areas of work, and the men and women active in them, should if possible be involved in planning the life of the congregation and setting its aims. Involving people in the running of the congregation is the only way to ensure that they are able and willing to represent it positively to the outside world.

Outside the congregation the first essential is a broad measure of tolerance and open-mindedness in dealing with the different groups in the district. If contacts and interchange are to develop, it is absolutely essential that all the different modes of living should be respected and taken seriously as attempts by human beings to cope with their existence. Great sensitivity is needed in introducing the dimension of religion into secular life, where the religious sense and the quest for meaning often lie deeply buried. The Christlike has to be recognized and put into words in its most varied garbs. Concretely, the gospel mission means accompanying people as they discover and work through their personal faith in the reality in which they live.

3. Good ideas can pay off only if they get good publicity. Church work must learn how to give itself a public profile. For this it needs an attractive, unusual, "unchurchy" get-up and an outgoing, inclusive approach on the part of its representatives. A wide variety of contacts inside and outside the congregation (including the press) must be sought and cultivated.

4. Last but not least, plans do not fall ready-made from heaven. Usually one discovers them gradually by reflecting systematically on what one has been doing almost intuitively for some time. The ideas set out here were not at first so consistently logical as they may appear, but have emerged and continue to emerge in the course of action and reflection. What has been said here is not the last word of wisdom but simply a stimulus for reflection.

ST TIKHON, MOSCOW, RUSSIA
The Orthodox Charitable Brotherhood

Sergey Chapnin

For the parishioners of the Church of St Tikhon and members of the Orthodox Charitable Brotherhood, January 17, 1990, will always remain an unforgettable day filled with a special paschal joy. On that winter day, the divine liturgy was celebrated in this cold and ruined church for the first time after sixty long years of desolation. This is how our community was born, when we began restoring the church not only as a stone temple, but also the temple of our hearts. St Tikhon, patriarch of Moscow and All Russia, was the first among those canonized as new martyrs of Russia, and our church was the first to be dedicated to a new martyr, as well as the first church to be returned to the Russian Orthodox Church in Klin County of Moscow Region.

According to Fr Sofrony Sakharov,

> Divine Providence has given the Russian church an experience of confession and martyrdom. Marxist humanism was merciless in its struggle against belief in God, and no sacrifices, no love, could overcome the embittered persecution pursued by the Bolsheviks. The Russian church has been utterly exhausted by suffering for the name of Christ. And this fact leads us as the Russian church to raise the question of perfection, prompted by the eternal spiritual law according to which perfection is preceded by full exhaustion.

How shall we order church life to achieve, even in a small degree, the tremendous task indicated by Father Sofrony? How do we understand perfection? Our prayer, search and reflection led us to form St Tikhon's Orthodox Charitable Brotherhood. Our choice of patron saint was not just an homage to the tradition according to which a brotherhood chooses the same saint as the church of which it is a part. Rather, it is a recognition of St Tikhon as a man of prayer and wise hierarch who has become a symbol of the lost unity of the Russian Orthodox Church.

Our brotherhood was created in January 1991 for common missionary, catechetical and charitable work. Among its members are those who live in Klin and nearby villages, as well as Muscovites, including parishioners of a number of churches in Moscow. The local Society of Spiritual Education, which brings together Orthodox teachers from state general education schools, is a corporate member.

In the very beginning we were only ten people, all parishioners of St Tikhon's, intuitively seeking to combine our efforts without a clear idea of how or — frankly speaking — even why. Had we been asked about our tasks at that time, we could hardly have articulated them. Today, however, we can see that we were right to do what we did. No brotherhood can be formed "from above"; it has to be born. A religious association whose task is to serve God cannot be a merely accidental grouping of people. It is called to be a union of love, a union of many in order to grow together internally, consolidating in truth. Any religious cause, however lofty it may be, is only "sounding brass or tinkling cymbal" if it lacks love.

Among the remaining vestiges of scholastic theology is the opinion that church work is the province of the clergy alone and that the laity, due to their status, should be spared all care for the church and active participation in its affairs. We believe that church work is a common task to be undertaken by every member, though the forms and means of church work should be differently distributed among clergy and laity. On this basis a living brotherhood has grown from a group of active parishioners, expressing the awareness — more a feeling at first — that it provides something which replenishes what is missing in a group of like-minded people, namely, churchliness, and what is missing in the parish today, namely, diakonia.

Our brotherhood is neither an assembly of intellectuals nor an elite. Each person finds a place according to his or her abilities and the needs of the brotherhood and the parish. The brotherhood's self-discipline and cohesion, as a manifestation of "the union of charity" to which every Christian community should aspire, may provoke suspicion from the outside. But the impression of a self-contained and isolated community vanishes at a closer look. A testimony to this is the continuous growth of Orthodox brotherhoods as new members come, attracted by their example of common service.

In affirming the need for missionary and catechetical work in Russia today, we face a paradoxical situation in which masses of people, though acquainted with Christ and connected with Christian culture, have no truly spiritual idea of Christ and his church at all or have an idea which is primitive, superficial and simply superstitious.

The church is being awakened to its mission. And we seek to use every opportunity to bear witness to Christ, to a life according to the precepts of the gospel and the spiritual experience of Orthodox Christians. Although the brotherhood is an organization of Orthodox Christians, we try to involve non-churched people who may have confidence in the church but do not think seriously about the spiritual foundations of life. Work in the brotherhood gives a person an excellent opportunity to participate in the life of a Christian community, rather than to judge it from the outside. For us this is a new and important way of missionary work.

In our missionary efforts we draw on the experience of the church. Our principal witness is the divine liturgy. Our brotherhood does not practice traditional common prayers because we live far from one another. It is the Sunday service that brings all our members together. The basis of our brotherhood's unity is the eucharistic fellowship.

Since its inception, the brotherhood has been engaged in Christian preaching through the mass media. In 1991 the parish published its own newspaper called *Our Church*; today the brotherhood prepares a monthly Orthodox page called *The Ark* for the district newspaper, with a circulation of 20,000 copies, and is regularly on the air through the local radio station.

The brotherhood's publishing house was established in 1992 as one of many ways of missionary and educational work. It is our conviction that the Russian Orthodox Church does not need reprinted editions which reduce Orthodoxy to the level of a museum piece or an archaeological curiosity. We seek to publish modern reference books on theology, accessible in language and style as well price to young people.

For over two years our church has been running a choral school, to which 60 children from 6 to 14 come twice a week. The 12 teachers also organize pilgrimages for children to various monasteries. In 1993 the brotherhood ran its first summer camp, called "A Little Seed". Among other new traditions which have been established are Christmas and Easter readings attended by children together with their parents and common festal meals. The brotherhood has arranged children's choir performances at homes for the elderly, as well as the church's regular choir recitals. It has organized tours for the children's and adults' theatres from the Church of Elijah the Prophet in Moscow, as well as lectures and exhibitions in local schools.

With the help of the World Council of Churches, the brotherhood has managed to open a small soup-kitchen to feed 20 children from low-income families whose names are provided by the local social welfare department. The community of the church and the brotherhood have participated in distributing humanitarian aid.

Several women members of our brotherhood have set up a sewing workshop. They restore old vestments and sew new ones, not only for our own church but also for other communities. We also plan to open a school of icon-painting. For us, restoration of the traditions of icon-painting, church music and sewing is not a nostalgic pursuit of the "good old days" but a way of bearing witness to the revival of the liturgical life of the church and its theology in prayer and ritual.

For over a year the brotherhood has also been operating a computer service. Our engineers repair second-hand computers and give them out to churches and hospitals.

Our brotherhood and parish have maintained fraternal relations with the community of the Church of St Nicholas in Bethlehem, Pennsylvania, USA, and the Lutheran parish of St Jacob in Wittlohe, Germany. From its first years, we have conducted international summer camps in which Russian, German, American and French people can work and relax together. We cherish these encounters, which help us to see anew the world around us and to come to a better knowledge of our neighbours and our own people and their faith.

Our ultimate goal — still only a dream — is to create a missionary centre to unite and coordinate all the work of the various units of the brotherhood. To implement this we hope to construct a special building to house a gymnasium, guest rooms and workshops.

The church must be awake to the needs of mission and create new bodies for missionary work, taking into account the realities of the world today. A key to fulfilling this task is an adequate organization of the parish life and missionary work of every community. It is our conviction that in our time, which is similar to the apostolic times, a missionary centre, whether like ours or organized differently, will become an integral part of the Christian community living life in its fullness.

4. Communicating Hope

A bruised reed he will not break,
and a dimly burning wick he will not quench;
he will faithfully bring forth justice... (Isa. 42:3).

Always be ready to make your defense to anyone who demands from
you an accounting for the hope that is in you (1 Pet. 3:15).

Abundant situations exist which seem to say "No hope". Each
of these is a challenge to the congregation to overcome attitudes of
hopelessness and to practise faith by communicating hope.

The beginning might be small yet of strategic importance: to
remove the litter and repair the windows in an almost abandoned
church and thus to demonstrate: this house of hope is being used.
Such a gesture may show people who see themselves as abandoned
that their situation matters to others, that they count.

The examples of congregations in this chapter show that
various factors can help to transform the mood of an entire
community from resignation to new hope, a hope grown out of
faith.

- Who are the people without hope that you know?
- How does your congregation seek to communicate hope to
  them?
- How are the language, gestures and images in your worship life
  celebrating hope?

PENRHYS, SOUTH WALES

A Well in the Wilderness

Donald Elliott

South Wales has been the scene of sweeping industrial and social changes. The entire economic base has shifted from the heavy industries of coal-mining and steel to brave attempts at diversification. Large-scale unemployment and disorientation have resulted.

Early in the 1960s the coal industry in South Wales was still thought to have an expanding future, unlike the North-East of England. To attract miners from the North-East, the idea of building a self-contained community 350 metres up in the coal valleys was conceived, and modern Penrhys was born. It might have been better if it had miscarried. By the time the 900 dwellings were finished, the coal industry had begun its decline and certainly no extra miners were needed.

Nobody wanted to go and live in Penrhys. Its location up in the clouds and winds is bleak and access is difficult. The poorly built houses soon showed signs of damp and cold. It became an estate to which only those desperate for housing would go, a last resort for the local authority. Unemployment is 84 percent, those receiving housing subsidy are 90 percent, and a large proportion of the 3500 residents live in single parent families. Thirty-seven percent of the population is under 14. With two percent of the population of the Rhondda district, Penrhys accounts for forty percent of its social welfare caseload.

As often happens in such situations, the frustrations of the people work themselves out in attacks on the public amenities. So the primary school has to be protected by a high wire fence, and the shopping centre has been so vandalized that only one store remains.

However, the local authority and the churches are now investing time and money. The council is having the houses upgraded, with fresh weather-proofing and economical heating. And the churches — from eight denominations — have joined to support a united ministry and the creation of a beautiful community centre and new church out of one of the less desirable housing blocks. It was opened on 29 February 1992.

The congregation, founded in 1971, became the Penrhys Uniting Church in 1989. Religiously, the context is one of decline. In 1914, nearby Tylorstown had eight chapels with 2000 worshippers. Today there are three chapels and 40 worshippers. (Then there were 4000 miners; now there are none.) Penrhys is an historic religious site. From the early Middle Ages until the Reformation, the ancient Celtic well and mediaeval Marian shrine were among the most famous sites of pilgrimage throughout southern Britain, celebrated in poem and song. The shrine, destroyed in 1538, was restored in 1953. The interest of the wider church is symbolized in the new building by an icon presented by a Welsh community of the Orthodox Church and by a bell given by the monks of the Roman Catholic Cistercian Order based at Caldy Island, Wales.

The current minister, John Morgans, has been helping the people to develop a theology rooted in their own lives, histories and experience. At the same time, local people contributed to the design of the community centre and now to its functioning. It is named Llanfair. In particular, many of the young women are thrilled to have a place to meet, bring their toddlers, do their laundry and have a good meal or a cup of tea. As a result of hard work and imagination, money for Llanfair has come from a variety of sources.

These are early days for the centre, but within its small compass various programmes have been started by the people. Apart from the launderette, creche and cafe, there is a boutique where "nearly new" clothes are sold. There is a knitting project which, it is hoped, will develop skills and even generate income. A library awaits the appointment of a literacy worker. And there is a minibus, which presently runs at a loss, but with increasing use may become viable.

Since 1989 the worshipping congregation has grown from 10 adults to about 50 adults and 50 children each Sunday. The development of "user-friendly" liturgies has been very important. Members of the congregation take turns to read, enter into discussion and offer names and themes for prayer. Twenty people will take an active role in a typical service. "Tailor-made" liturgies are designed for weddings and funerals, which become events for the whole community.

Remarkably for a rather non-literate community, Paul's letter to the Romans has been the basis for preparation of adults for baptism. The key has been the use of an interpretative translation of the Bible designed for schools (Alan Dale's) and a study method which helps people to find themselves and their own experience and insight, as well as God, within the biblical account.

The church's long-term aim is to help residents feel pride in themselves and have stability in their community. For this to happen, the people of Penrhys will have to be involved in creatively changing both the reality and the image of their situation. They will need to develop partnerships with others, including businesses, statutory authorities and churches.

One development scheme in the making is to attract visitors to celebrate the Penrhys heritage. Already the Uniting Church has written and performed an Easter play to audiences totalling 750 people. It is feasible that a community celebration combining a mediaeval miracle play and soap opera could attract really large numbers. A modest amphitheatre has been suggested. Another idea is to develop a pilgrimage route from the Marian shrine up through the township to the nearest hilltop, which offers spectacular views.

The church is also aware of some of the long-term issues that have to be probed and addressed: attitudes to work and employment training; attitudes to property (ownership versus dependency); security in the struggle against crime and vandalism; education for self-worth and community values; leisure needs and facilities.

VALDOSENDE, PORTUGAL

A Story of Change and Hope

Maria Eunice M. Alves

Valdosende is a small mountain village in the north of Portugal. The nearest town is Braga, about 35 km. away.

In the early 1970s, when this story begins, Valdosende had around 300 inhabitants, most of whom lived on subsistence farming.

Though it was a tiny spot on the map, Valdosende made news in the local and national press in 1971, when it decided to ask the Methodist Church in Portugal to come and stay in the village.

It is difficult to explain objectively the reasons for this enormous change in the villagers' lives at that time, involving the abandonment of their religious and social background. If we go back to 1971, we learn that a large power station had started to function a few kilometers away, but Valdosende and other nearby villages were not immediately provided with electricity. Other basic services were also lacking: irrigation, better roads, sewage, medical assistance, good educational facilities. Combined with all this was the fact that the local Catholic priest had decided, without consulting the population, to leave the village, close the historic old church and build a new one a few kilometres away. All this provoked a feeling of loneliness and almost despair in the people of Valdosende.

Finally, tired of seeing their religious rights so rudely neglected and feeling ignored by the Catholic hierarchy, the people took a difficult but decisive step: they asked the Methodist church in Braga to come to the village and give them religious assistance because they "could not live without God and needed guidance in the way of the faith". Thus emerged "a Protestant island in a Catholic sea", to use the title of a national newspaper article in October 1971.

Without any form of proselytism but by invitation of the people of Valdosende, the Methodist church started its work preaching reconciliation through God's love revealed in Jesus Christ and became involved in changing the villagers' lives. This impulse came from the same God who is constantly helping the church to learn anew what he expects from it wherever it is placed.

Attentive to the characteristics of the villagers, the Methodists encouraged a community spirit; and when the time came, the whole population committed itself to building a Methodist temple through volunteer work and to support the social work undertaken by the church, which continues to this day.

A common tradition in this region is a spring festival celebrated by each village, normally with the patronage of a local saint. In Valdosende, this tradition was re-created as a harvest festival, which takes place every autumn, a unique opportunity to show joy and gratitude for all that God has been doing. The festival takes an entire weekend. On Sunday there is a thanksgiving service, followed by a procession of gifts to be auctioned, with all the proceeds going to church activities, mostly diaconal. This is also an occasion for people to meet friends from villages nearby.

The diaconal project of the church has been an example for the region, showing the loving power of God at work in the village. Considering the village's limited human and material resources, it is extensive and quite demanding.

The project was set up almost immediately after the establishment of the Methodist church in the village. A kindergarten was opened with the help of some churches and friends abroad. Little children, who had normally been left alone at home when their mothers had to work in the fields, found a place of refuge and joy which also contributed to their future development. A nursery was also opened. Health assistance was provided by a doctor and dentist who visited the village monthly. Today, a nearby government medical centre provides health care so the local Methodist community maintains only the regular visits of the dentist.

In 1980 a rural development project was set up with support from the Dutch Reformed Church. New forms of agriculture were tested and implemented, and a herd of goats, belonging to the whole population, was created. This project has now developed into a cooperative which aims to be self-supporting in the near future with the active contribution of all its members, who include the great majority of the resident families.

The social witness of the church in Valdosende has now been extended to young people by the opening of a students' home in Braga and to the elderly by establishment of a day centre where they can have meals and enjoy activities together.

All these intensive social activities follow a common strategy: to be a congregation which tries, despite its ups and downs, to link the loving and liberating *word* of God with *action* coming from all God's people.

We need more trained people to meet the needs of the people inside and outside Valdosende. We also dream of new forms of ministry more adapted to the changing situations of the people. Many young people leave the village to work in other parts of Europe as migrants, and we feel they are needed here. Confronted and challenged by the persistence of this phenomenon, we wonder if we will be ready one day — through faith and hope — to contribute once more to the economic and spiritual development of this region, helping to create new jobs which will motivate these people to remain in their own beloved land.

We believe that this vision, which we have cherished for a long time, is inspired by the same God in whom we have been putting our trust. He is always giving us new opportunities to take the future in our own hands and shape it anew for his glory and the benefit of humankind.

CONISBROUGH, SOUTH YORKSHIRE, ENGLAND

Communicating Hope against Despair

David Sherwin

Conisbrough, in the county of South Yorkshire, England, has a long history. The Anglican church of St Peter dates back to the eighth century, the castle to the twelfth. The population remained around 400 until the nineteenth century when Denaby and Cadeby coal mines were sunk, and it reached 17,500 in the 1960s; but since then, after the closing of the two mines, it has decreased to about 12,500. Unemployment has risen sharply, with no major employer filling the void left by the closing of the pits. The people originate from Scotland, Newcastle and Yorkshire; there are very few people of other colour or race. Socially, they are mainly working class (but without work), although there are some who aspire to the middle class.

Apart from St Peter's there are Baptist and Methodist congregations in our parish, and Catholic and Salvation Army congregations in a neighbouring parish. When Ian Chrisholm became vicar of St Peter's in 1976, he inherited a congregation of about 35 people. During his early years he sought to give consistent biblical teaching and to get the church and its community buildings into a good state of repair to counteract a widespread mood of resignation. When I arrived as a lay evangelist in 1986, the church had grown to a membership of around 250. This growth was due to the renewal of the church through the vicar's influence, the impact of Mission Sheffield, led by evangelist Billy Graham, and the effect of the teaching of John Wimber, which released many members into new areas of service in the power of the Holy Spirit. Basically the church had renewed its confidence in the gospel it was given to share, and the members had a new expectation of what God could do in their lives and the lives of others.

During this time there had also been much change and uncertainty in the social situation. Industrial action in 1985 to "save" the pits seemed to have been in vain, as the government pressed on with streamlining the mining industry, which meant closing mines in the area. In the midst of all this, the congregation sought God's guidance in prayer. As the people prayed, God revealed that they were not forgotten, that he would act by transforming the lives of the people as they responded to the good news of Jesus and that this transformation would affect the whole community, people and land.

My part in this has been to develop an evangelistic strategy to enable the people to share their faith within the community and help others to see the relevance of Christ to themselves.

First we set up a prayer strategy, called "lights on every street", to enable the whole church to play its part in living out the Christian responsibility to pray for all people. Each person was given a prayer card to enable praying for those living on their street. Told to be a "praying, caring, and sharing people", they have done and still do this with great enthusiasm. To enable the caring to happen several activities are organized by the laity: a second-hand clothing shop called Steptoes, a family group, a group for pre-school children and their parents and guardians, and Highway, a skill centre for the unemployed and others with time on their hands. To encourage sharing, training is given on how to share one's journey of faith and guest services are organized to which they can bring their friends, knowing they will hear the gospel presented in a culturally relevant way.

During the first three years of this scheme we added more than a hundred people to the church. Many people saw friends and relatives come to or return to faith. When we relaunched the scheme after the first three years, the influx of new people seemed to slow down. The plateau in church growth may have been due to the fact that the people prayed for during the first three years were already "on the fringe" of the church and were the most natural to come in first. So we needed something to enable a new "fringe" to be built. This led to the arrival of "Barney the Bus", a 1951 London double-decker bus.

The idea was that by taking the church to the community we would be able to forge links with people now outside the church with whom we had very little contact. The bus, after some modifications, provided us with a portable building on wheels. The lower deck was converted into a refreshment lounge; upstairs, all seats were removed and the floor carpeted, with portable seats available when needed. We also made a removable puppet theatre for use upstairs. Once the interior and exterior modifications were made and it was mechanically checked, we were ready to go out into the community.

We looked for roads where the bus could be parked in a strategic position for visits to surrounding homes. Our first experience was outside some flats for senior citizens. As soon as we arrived, they came out to meet us. They made cakes, gave us donations for the bus and enjoyed sitting on the bus for long periods of the day, talking to us. We shared our faith with them on a one-to-one level and also held formal services on board. Upstairs we would set up chairs and an organ. Those who came enjoyed the singing, gave requests for prayer and responded to what was shared with them about the Christian faith.

Due to the enthusiasm with which these folk gave us their prayer requests, we decided to introduce a visitation programme taking this into consideration, asking people in the area how we could pray for them and share more of Christ with them. While the bus was parked, some would stay on board to welcome visitors inside for a drink, while others went out to each household, letting people know that the church cared about them, sharing our faith with them and collecting prayer requests. Many of the requests concerned those who were sick; others asked us to pray that they would get a job. One man who asked this had a job within a week — but then the message came back saying, "Thank you, but it is not the job I wanted. Could you pray for a different one?"

We divided the parish into areas of about 100 homes and visited area by area. This strategy has brought a growing number of people into contact with the church who would otherwise not have been reached. While the challenge to follow Christ further is in their hands, we continue to keep in touch with them through follow-up visits. This has been one area of apparent failure due to a number of circumstances. Keeping in touch with these people is difficult, as is taking them further in their faith: we found that after visiting over 700 households only 80 wished for further contact.

In every area the bus visits we try to run a special programme for the children, usually after school hours. The "Kids Hour" consists of singing, a short video of a Bible story, a quiz or board game, refreshments, a puppet show (usually a parable) and sometimes other activities. At the end each child is given a sticker with a Christian motif and a leaflet for parents explaining the various church activities.

Since the children's Bible knowledge is usually minimal, we try to teach them the stories in a lively and interesting way, not just so they can answer questions about them but so that they can apply the Christian teachings to their lives. What we do with and for the children is received very well by them and their parents.

A more specialized use of the bus is with children in schools, with the approval of the head teacher. On such a visit we are allowed to have one class for a period of 30-40 minutes. During this time the children are given a brief introduction on the development of buses, explaining how they have changed in design and use over the years. This leads naturally to an explanation of what we do with our bus, and they are then given a condensed version of what we do on the streets. The puppet show on this occasion is about Barnabas, the Bible character after whom the vehicle is named. At the end of the lesson, the children are given a sticker and a cardboard model of the bus, which they can put together. The staff and children appreciate this lesson greatly, and school-church links have been greatly improved by this venture.

Teenagers are also given their own special times on the bus. We have tried various ideas: board games, video games, Christian videos, music, lighting effects, discussion groups and a variety of open-air evangelistic presentations. Having tried all these things to help us get alongside young people, it would seem that all we require is loud music — and readiness to talk to them over it!

The prayer strategy and the work of Barney the bus continue; and there is still much work to be done. One lady summed up the effect of the work in the parish: "Why hasn't the bus been on our street lately? We miss you when you don't come. The last time you came, I was left with a lot of questions, but I also felt good. Please come again soon."

Within all this busy strategy it needs to be said that nothing replaces the personal encounters we have with people and the opportunities these encounters give us for Christ. St Peter's now sees approximately 600 people attending services every month. Of these, 400 make up the regular weekly core. The growth is given by God, for which we praise him, but he also expects us to work for that growth and be committed to the work of building his church.

SMOLENSK, RUSSIA

An Orthodox Children's Theatre

Iwna Lisovskay

For many years, the life of Orthodox parishes in Russia was largely confined within the walls of the churches, and the faces of children or young people were rarely seen. Now, churches and parishes are becoming centres of spiritual life for most believers, including youth and children.

In Smolensk, an old city in the central European part of Russia, an Orthodox children's theatre has become one of the vivid manifestations of community life. It appeared in 1989, and among its first actors were children who attended the Sunday school of the Cathedral of the Dormition. The previous year had seen the millennium of the Baptism of Russia become a national celebration, testifying to a new openness towards the church in society. In 1989 the first parish Sunday schools appeared. And in this movement shaping parishes as centres of spiritual life, Smolensk occupies a prominent place, for the head of the diocese, Metropolitan Kirill, has been able to overcome the inertia of traditionalists and sceptics and support the initiatives of those who wished to change life in parishes.

There are 120 children, from 4 to 16, involved in the Orthodox children's theatre in Smolensk. They are pupils of the Sunday school, the Orthodox kindergarten and the gymnasium. The theatre stages five plays a year, normally timed for the great events on the church calendar: the beginning of the Christmas fast, Christmas, Christmas-tide (the period between Christmas and Epiphany), Shrove-tide (before Lent) and Easter.

The origins of Russian theatre and its best traditions go back to the eleventh century when scenery representing a furnace was installed in the church before Christmas. A "furnace drama" was enacted around the story of the Chaldean conspiracy against the three young Jewish men who refused to worship the golden image set up by Nebuchadnezzar (Daniel 3). Later the church, out of concern for a moral Christian way of life, abandoned theatre and any staging of drama. But like the prodigal son, the theatre was to return to the church. In the seventeenth century, Simenon of Polotsk, a monk and schoolteacher, laid the foundation of the Orthodox school theatre for biblical drama. In 1728, a school theatre was opened in the seminary in Smolensk. First it adapted religious rites for the stage, then presented plays. Between 1752 and 1754 it staged plays written by Bazilevich, a teacher at the seminary.

The main task of the Orthodox children's theatre in Smolensk is to educate children ethically and artistically. The theatre has in its repertoire all the surviving comedies by Simenon of Polotsk, as well as plays with biblical plots, among them "On Joseph", "Ahasuerus's Drama" and "Holofernes's Drama". A distinctive feature of the Smolensk theatre are presentations that combine puppets and acting, as in "King Herod". There are also scenes written by the children themselves, such as "The Tale of a Proud Rose" and "The First Red Egg".

Using their imagination and writing have a great impact on the development of children, helping them to think in images, strengthening their memory and unfolding their creative abilities. But the most important result is that young children learn to communicate with one another — and not only on the stage. Perhaps this is the most difficult thing to do in life, and our theatre is making its own contribution to solving this problem.

Theatre is creativity addressed to people. Wherever children perform, whether in the large hall of a theatre, in a tiny ward in a hospital or home for the elderly, in a kindergarten, in a rural community club or in a library, their creativity meets with a lively response. They come out to meet people, presenting lessons of morality, goodness, mercy and beauty and opening their hearts to them to show light, love and their childlike faith.

Christmas celebrations in Smolensk began with a major festive performance by the children at the regional theatre on 7 January, the day when the Orthodox in Russia celebrate Christmas. They acted out several biblical scenes, sang and conducted a Christmas quiz for the spectators. After Christmas come the holidays called *Sviatki*, a time of universal festivities when people greet one another after a long fast. Following the old custom, children came out into the streets to sing Christmas carols interspersed with humorous catch-phrases and greetings "to glorify the newly born infant Christ". Traditionally, this is a time for visiting the sick, the needy and prisoners. Every day was marked with a visit to a hospital, where the children gave performances, sang, distributed presents and treated the sick to sweets. During the last day of the Christmas holidays, the children of the Orthodox theatre visited a prison and performed for the inmates, many of whose eyes were moist as they watched "The Furnace Drama". After the performance, the children gave out copies of the gospels and sweets.

The children glorified Christ throughout the city — at factories, offices, schools, kindergartens, market places, railway stations, homes for the elderly and orphanages. No one was left indifferent. They brought the gifts of their hearts and the present of sweets, and they were given presents and gifts of the heart in return. When asked where they had liked to perform best — their sponsors' enterprise, where they were given presents, or in the hospital, where they themselves gave out sweets — they answered that they liked it best in the hospital. It was more important for them to give than to receive.

Things are not always smooth at the theatre. Those accustomed to more traditional forms of parish life do not always understand how it is possible to sing and dance and change clothes and act inside the church. It has taken time to cleanse people's eyes and hearts of the spiritual scars and hardness which shun the light of joy that is Christmas in Smolensk, the birth of new life and new hope.

5. The Healing Gospel

But Peter said, "I have no silver or gold, but what I have I give you; in the name of Jesus Christ of Nazareth, stand up and walk" (Acts 3:6).

Are any among you sick? They should call for the elders of the church and have them pray over them, anointing them with oil in the name of the Lord. The prayer of faith will save the sick, and the Lord will raise them up (James 5:14-15).

The gospel is relevant for all realms of life as well as for the wholeness of life. The healing ministry of Christ aims at the restitution of all brokenness and the overcoming of all evil forces.

Christian communities are given the power of the Spirit to participate in Christ's healing ministry today through liberating people from bondage or through overcoming evil with good (Rom. 12:21).

- What are the illnesses and fragmentations which cry for healing in the neighbourhood of your congregation?
- How is your congregation participating in the healing ministry of Christ?
- How does your congregation enable people to contribute to the healing dimension of faith in counselling, visiting and sharing?

RADOTIN, CZECH REPUBLIC

The Church as a Healing Community

Miroslav Heryan

Just as Jesus Christ used his body in acts of service and healing —
travelling from place to place to preach the kingdom of God and heal the
outcast and the blind by his touch — so, too, the Lord needs the "body" of
his church to spread his gospel and bring his help to those in need
"between the ages". Jesus left behind the church in this world to manifest
his existence and his service. The church thus participates in Christ's
struggle against the powers of evil. All this we know from the Bible, but
from time to time we have an unexpected *experience* which brings the full
truth of it home to us.

Radotin is a suburb of Prague. A small congregation of the Evangelical Church of the Czech Brethren has existed there since 1941. Cernosice
— itself outside Prague city limits — also belongs to this parish. Many
residents of both places commute daily to Prague to work.

The beginnings of this Protestant congregation date back to the years
immediately after the first world war, which witnessed a movement
"away from Rome". But only a few of these founding families were able
to pass on the faith to their children and grandchildren; and under
communism the congregation almost disappeared. Radotin's strong communist tradition had an effect on the churches: the Catholic parsonage
was requisitioned and a Protestant pastor lost his licence because he
had studied in the USA. The hopes raised during the "Prague Spring" of
1968 were soon snuffed out by the invasion of Warsaw Pact forces on
21 August of that year.

While almost everyone seemed paralyzed by fear and apathy, the
pastor who arrived in the parish at the time was full of drive, inspired by
ecumenical meetings he had attended. He was enthusiastic about team
work in the congregation, about the "missionary congregation" and about
local ecumenism. But with whom could he share or realize his ideas?

New people came only slowly, as a result of resettling, repeated
invitation, friendly contacts, the search for a home — all this in answer to
much prayer. The congregation started to grow. An ecumenical house
group was formed and later became the support group for congregational
renewal. To date, six such house groups have been formed in the two
places. Some display a charismatic spirituality, though such groups see
themselves as serving the whole congregation and do not try to force their

brand of spirituality on others. This growth in spirit and in numbers prepared for the many new opportunities arising after the political changes of 1989.

Renewal began with a case of need. A local Christian family adopted Pauline, a 12-year-old girl from an institution for "problem children". A well-known Christian psychologist had described the child as incorrigible and beyond redemption. By that age she was already experimenting with drugs and had made several attempts to run away from the home. She was also epileptic.

This Christian family tried everything: love, care and discipline. Pauline was even confirmed in the church, but her actions and reactions continued to be unpredictable. Finally, at the age of 16, she was entrusted to the care of a young married couple (he a theologian and she a psychologist). That is how she came into our church.

At the beginning there was great hope. Pauline was received by the young people and by some families with great affection, and she was happy to have so many kind-hearted "aunts" and "uncles". But soon she made new contacts in bars, among heavy metal musicians, satanists and, again, drug dealers. Twice she had to be sought by the police, but even after that she was still surrounded with great love. She was taken in by three families.

It was clear to us that love was not enough, that we had to seek God's intervention. After much prayer a celebration was organized — Pauline *came of age*. She had had another relapse not long before, but now she wanted to break with all her bad connections. In a prayer of commitment she acknowledged her rebellion as sinful and repented. With the laying on of hands she was solemnly granted full forgiveness and freedom in the blood of Jesus.

Today Pauline is the mother of two healthy children. Three years have gone by, which represent a successful probationary period. The congregation has seen the change, though only very few really know what had taken place. We had learned an important lesson: the love of Christ and the power of the Holy Spirit are needed to heal deep wounds. Christ's love attracts those who are in need, the power of the Spirit brings about change and abiding love secures the whole.

As new members continue to come to our congregation, we discover new tasks. Many of these people feel they lack something, which they hope to find among us:

• Some come seeking a solution for family tensions. The congregation includes several young families who can look back at crises now overcome. These "healed" families are the ones who are now ready to help others.

• More and more people arrive looking for work. We have been able to help some of them by joining with them in their search.

• A young man took to alcohol because he could see no solution to his problems. Two young men in the congregation who had been freed from alcohol by God's power are now trying to help this young man give up drinking.

• A ten-year-old girl attempted suicide at school because she could no longer endure her depressing home situation: her father was a heavy drinker; her mother had abandoned the home. The girl's life was saved. Now she has found real love within a family of our congregation.

• A young man with advanced leukaemia, a former Communist Party member, now attends church services. His mother had been regularly visited by members of our congregation throughout her long terminal illness. He now wishes to take over the torch of faith.

• A former Jehovah's Witness came to us asking to be admitted into our congregation as he had really found Jesus there. His arrival was followed by that of other former Witnesses.

We continue to discover much human need around us. In some cases we try to help; in others we are powerless. But in many cases which come to us or which we come across in the area, we discover unsuspected *abilities*, which had previously remained buried and untapped. In this way we help to build up the body of Christ in our congregation.

At the same time we are also discovering that above and beyond denominational boundaries we Christians need each other to make us better able to serve and lend assistance.

In Cernosice, where none of the different denominations owns a church building, an ecumenical group known as "The Christians of Cernosice" has been issuing invitations to ecumenical worship in secular premises since 1989.

On Easter Monday 1990 the popular Catholic priest Vaclav Maly spoke to a packed conference room at the Cernosice Hotel about what the cross and Christ's open tomb mean to him. I spoke on the euphoria over the end of the totalitarian system and the fact that even after the change people have remained the same. New human beings are needed for a new future. It is Jesus who will make us new. The following day we received a telephone call from the citizens' group urging us to continue our work: "We need Christ's message. Keep coming to neutral ground, since many people are hesitant about entering a church."

Since then we have been holding monthly Christian seminars in the school hall. We are trying to find ways to reach people who have never been in a church. The ecumenical support group is preparing the programme. It also produces ideas for local social and humanitarian work and has taken the initiative in ecumenical work with children and young people. Group members carry over the impetus from this ecumenical work to their three congregations, thus fostering the "ecumenical renewal of congregations".

SHEFFIELD, ENGLAND

The Nine O'Clock Service

Walking into one of the weekly services at Ponds Forge in the city centre of Sheffield, England, you are confronted by an ever-expanding series of concentric circles. A circular table, which appears at first to be the sun and the crescent moon, in fact portrays an eclipse — the new creation emerging out of the old. The table is in the centre of a ring of pillars, and hundreds of people gather in the circular underground chamber to hear and experience the word of God. All of this is a visual analogy of the planet we inhabit and of the curved nature of the universe, designed to join with the powerful re-emergence of awe, mysticism and natural theology which is starting to take place.

In this picture, the sacraments are at the epicentre of a "New Big Bang", with ripples of life-force spreading out like shock-waves. Massive video screens continually feed images of nature, the universe and humanity. It is a sea of paradox — high tech, but with the ambience of an ancient crypt. It is designed to be a place where rhythm, meditation, dance and light can reconnect people with God, transforming their vision of the world. This is the Nine O'Clock Service's "Planetary Mass", and the central core of our existence as a eucharistic community.

The service is intended to be an interpretative symbol for the reality of the worship already happening in creation. The whole universe is invited to an intimate event — the feasting on the cosmic Christ. In a sense the church has no walls: we worship with and on behalf of plants and planets, animals and angels, celebrating Christ as the origin, the Alpha, the source of all creation. The local community in the context of the great cosmic community, aware of its limitations and straining towards its fulfilment in Christ, sees in him the hope of wholeness and of freedom from sin and decay. Therefore, at the communion table we celebrate not only what is and what is to come but also becoming.

The Nine O'Clock Service is a nascent church, a community of people seeking to develop in practice an authentically Anglican church model, which has been given the freedom to experiment on behalf of the whole church within the boundaries that hold the Anglican Communion together. It is called the Nine O'Clock Service partly because 9:00 p.m. was the only time available to meet in the church building, and partly because it seemed the natural time for people from a "club culture" to get together to celebrate.

Started in 1986, it has grown rapidly. Numerically, it has expanded from a congregation of 60 people to one of over 500, whose average age is in the late twenties. In 1989 one hundred people were confirmed in a single service. The service has inspired many other groups and has been copied in dozens of places around the country. This growth has been centred on a group of artists and musicians who were on the fringes of the church or outside the Christian faith. They were at the heart of "house music" and multi-media experimentation in the early 1980s and were activists in social, political and environmental concern. This group formed a base community whose initial focus was a discovery of the practical implications of committed discipleship and the development of a just and sustainable life-style, which is now at the heart of the Nine O'Clock Service.

The church now attracts two main groups of people. For some, the search for God has already been taking place in the world, in their work in environmental and justice issues, which they are then able to redefine through Jesus Christ. They are often looking for a spirituality that their political activities lack. A second group is those who come to find healing — a personal wholeness that happens through social and spiritual healing in the community. There are also some "rebellious returnees" — Christians who because of cultural alienation reacted against the church, and have now been given a way back in. It is a mixture of people looking to continue their search for and find practical evidence of a vision that includes hope, community, healing for the planet, sexual justice and food for the starving, in an open, non-dogmatic atmosphere.

The church in the 1990s is in a completely new missionary situation. Through the power of modern technology and contemporary economic and political realities, a new global worldview is emerging. Our post-modern era has been united by current technologies into an instantaneous 24-hour information world. In the West there is a growing insistence that we must live in the present, with a plural and heterogeneous range of life-styles and viewpoints. In this multi-faith, multi-cultural, chaotic, "white noise" society, the church's traditional language and dogma are not heard, because the old ways of presenting them just do not work. Broadly speaking, 97 percent of the English population is outside the church.

Western culture is struggling to come to terms with new realities. Environmental catastrophe looms on the horizon. At the present rate of deforestation, the rain-forest will be destroyed in just fifty years, taking with it ecosystems which contain 90 percent of all the earth's wildlife species, which it has taken 18 thousand million years of creative process to produce. In the midst of ecological disaster and the decline of Western culture, whose addictive, destructive nature is being increasingly recognized, humanity is in pain. Millions in the Third World are starving and dying for the lack of basic necessities; and people in the West, in relative material affluence, are often in spiritual and psychological agony. The church seems irrelevant and indeed, to a growing percentage of young people, as part of the cause of the problems. The gospel is not being heard.

The Nine O'Clock Service endeavours to offer a non-dogmatic free choice, in which guilt and repression are lesser motivators and vision, life, freedom, justice, passion and excitement are real currency. Christian community in that context is a place where complacency is turned into compassion. We believe that religion freed from a reductionist, scientifically rationalized worldview and from the claustrophobic dogmas of the Enlightenment is critical in finding a new way forward. Surely this is the real charismatic movement.

The Nine O'Clock Service is open to anyone, including people of other faiths, to join us in celebration of life-force, whose ultimate source we as Christians see in Jesus. We see the Spirit of God at work in the world as people fight for justice, seek out truth and create beauty, but also at work in the universal church. The only way for us to draw these together and bridge the gap has been through a dynamic of oscillating between the two. The Spirit of God has again and again drawn us to where he is at work in the world, so that we can define that work in terms of Christ.

Universal language. The formation of language and the communication of truth within culture are directly linked. If we are to have the tools to communicate the gospel today, the participation of Christians at the forefront of the creation of culture and language is essential. There needs to be a rediscovery, in a secular sense, of many things in common language that in a more openly religious society would describe the reality of God. The Nine O'Clock Service is seeking to use a language that anyone, whether inside or outside the church, can understand, so that there is no split between "sacred" and "secular" language. For example, talk of the "Holy Spirit" is meaningless to many people, but terms like "the spirit of life" or "passion for living" will strike a chord in most people's experience.

The Nine O'Clock Service is working in a world where there is an increasingly open market of religions and beliefs, where Christianity will need to show up favourably in these "God" or "life" terms. However, in this apparently competitive environment, we believe that all faiths, including Christianity, need to be judged in the light of Christ. The discovery of how Christ is "a light to the Gentiles" in our modern world is a central part of the church's mission.

The new art. God has made us "co-creators". Creativity is a fundamental law of the human psyche, just as it is for the universe. To recover this sense that we are a special part of the living, dynamic whole, we need to release the locked-up creativity that is in every human soul, to re-value creativity as a moral virtue. By creativity we do not mean the modern concept of art as an objective consumer product — "art on the wall" — but rather the totality of creative humanity seen in the person of Jesus. This is not only expressed in compassion-led justice, but also in worship-making. Through visual spectacle, through the erotic realm of myth, symbol, poetry, song, dance and ritual, through the totality of human experience and emotion, body, mind and soul, we encounter the living God and express his nature in the world.

To do this we have drawn heavily on the deep resources found in our own Christian tradition and increasingly on the riches of other world faiths. Some of these allow us to re-participate with the body of nature, and encourage intimate communion with the natural world. The cyclical rhythms of natural seasons and festivals were at one time integral to church life. The significance of these festivals has largely been lost, but in regaining their meaning we can provide the community with a concrete way of understanding God that is not removed from nature and in ritual works out ways of addressing the cataclysmic problems facing our species. This is where the churches can help to move people towards the change of consciousness necessary within the entire human order.

The Nine O'Clock Service is struggling to work out new ways of living a religious life of faith in an emergency situation, and to reinterpret the neglected riches of the creation traditions with a renewed vision of redemption, not just to preserve the world but to co-create cultures that will take humanity and creation in Christ to eternal salvation. In this setting, the ritual of holy communion is lifeblood for recovery.

LISBURN, NORTHERN IRELAND
Raising Good Out of Evil

For almost 400 years, Roman Catholics and Protestants have lived side-by-side in Northern Ireland. But from time to time, violent conflicts have erupted. In earlier years, there was a considerable element of religious persecution of each side by the other, not unlike similar conflicts throughout Europe. In recent, more ecumenical times, Catholics and Protestants worthy of the name no longer persecute each other; but the increasingly inappropriate labels "Catholic" and "Protestant" still tend to be applied to opposing sides in the violence which continues to be perpetrated, and it has to be admitted that many of the people involved are nominal members of one denomination or the other. The reasons for the continuing outbreaks of violence are complex and difficult to explain but they are essentially political, related to such factors as cultural identity, social and economic deprivation, the partitioning of Ireland in 1921 and, it must not be overlooked, the working of the devil.

One thing is certain. Were it not for the fact that many Catholics and Protestants have come together in various successful cross-community initiatives such as Corrymeela, Cornerstone, Columbanus, Protestant and Catholic Encounter, Women Together and others, the violence would be on a much larger scale. Nevertheless, because of mutual fear and suspicion on the part of many others, such initiatives encompass only a small proportion of people of each denomination. Many still prefer to witness to Jesus Christ in the exclusive context of Catholicism or Protestantism, which falls short of the example set by our Lord and greatly weakens the condemnations of violence which Catholic and Protestant religious leaders regularly make in the name of Christ, thus negating a positive witness to reconciliation.

In Lisburn, a town of 42,000 people, the Presbyterian Church in the town centre has twice been badly damaged in recent years by Irish

Republican Army car bombs placed to destroy nearby shops and businesses. As well as structural damage to the building, all the beautiful stained glass windows were shattered. What a dismal, disheartening sight! However, with careful collection of the broken glass and the wonderful skill of the stained glass artist the windows were eventually replaced and returned to their former beauty, incorporating much of the original glass. But when many pieces of this glass could not be fitted into the newly made windows, a truly inspired plan was made and carried out. The left-over pieces of glass were used to create a new stained glass window with the theme of resurrection — the symbolic raising of good out of evil.

The window depicts a burst of light (like an explosion) radiating from an orb at its centre. It symbolizes the breaking down of old hatreds and prejudices and the rising up of a new understanding. This resurrection window also witnesses to the spirit of the people of Lisburn, who continue to conquer all adversity, and thus gives new pertinence to the motto of the town: *Ex igne resurgam* — "I shall arise from the fire" — a reference to the virtual destruction of Lisburn in an accidental fire in 1707. Above all, it testifies to our faith, to the living out of our belief that good can come out of evil and to the deep respect we have for others' beliefs.

The other churches in the town were very sympathetic and supportive after the destruction of the church building, donating money towards repairs and offering to share their buildings. The response of the Roman Catholic people to the plight of the Presbyterian congregation was spontaneous and generous and so impressed the minister, Gordon Gray, that he felt moved to lead his flock to embrace the local St Patrick's Roman Catholic Church, across the invisible barriers of suspicion, distrust, fear and misunderstanding with which the two communities had often regarded each other.

This was the impulse which led to the birth of our Cross-Community Group. This Group comprises lay people and clergy from both churches, who meet regularly with the chief purpose of building trust and understanding through friendship, discussion and working together. We feel that we have been led by the Holy Spirit to approach each other across the religious divide and to show our respect for one another's beliefs. We have worshipped together in our respective church buildings, held social events, raised money to further our interest in the wider community, participated in discussions about our differences and similarities and spent a residential weekend together which increased the bonds of friendship.

At this gathering, held in the peace and quiet of a rural Roman Catholic priory, we developed an atmosphere in which we were able to discuss contentious issues frankly and freely. Misconceptions and myths of both denominations were aired and corrected and we discussed what we perceived to be the positives and negatives of each. We attended worship in each other's churches on the Sunday — not a common occurrence in Northern Ireland today. At the close of our time together we all took part in an ecumenical act of worship which we had composed. The trust and understanding that developed and grew among us during this weekend increased our confidence in each other, and we became more comfortable one with another. We are now able to demonstrate this cohesion by going together to visit those people of both denominations in our community who have been bereaved due to violence. Atrocities have been carried out against both Roman Catholics and Protestants, and our hands and sympathy are extended to whoever is suffering.

We believe we are being used by God as a channel through which his peace may flow. The process is slow-moving, and our membership could be larger in number. We have been notably unsuccessful so far in involving the young people between 17 and 30 of our congregations in our activities. This is a failing but we are challenged by it and intend to address the issue.

Out of a violent situation, we have been led by the Holy Spirit to break down divisions and to unite with fellow Christians without feeling that we have compromised fundamental principles. We are aware of the Spirit's continued promptings to us to avail ourselves of every opportunity that presents itself so that we might go forward in peace and understanding.

6. Meeting Christ in the Wounded

Truly I tell you, just as you did it to one of the least of these who are members of my family, you did it to me (Matt. 25:40).

The chief priests…, along with the scribes and elders, were mocking him, saying, "He saved others; he cannot save himself. He is the King of Israel; let him come down from the cross now, and we will believe in him. He trusts in God; let God deliver him now, if he wants to" (Matt. 27:41-43).

Christ was wounded, Christ suffered — and thus he became the one who is near to those who are wounded, who are suffering today. He expects us to meet him in the wounded — the asylum-seekers and refugees, the homeless and jobless, the forgotten children.

Congregations that try to be open for wounded people, to live Christ's love by being at the side of those longing for love, often discover that they become receivers rather than givers.

- Where do you meet wounded people?
- Are we aware of our own bitterness and pain?
- How is your congregation meeting these realities?

LUKAS CHURCH, GELSENKIRCHEN, GERMANY
Christians and Asylum
Rolf Heinrich

Willingness to offer sanctuary to refugees is not created by information meetings, "refugee days", or even cultural events at which we share each other's traditions, customs and food. In the congregation of the Lukas Church in Gelsenkirchen, Germany, we came to offer asylum after sixteen years of trying to share in the day-to-day problems of the people in our district of the city and to understand them as an integral part of our church life. We learned that the Christian community is a place where people who feel isolated and powerless as individuals can join together and encourage one another rather than simply accepting their suffering passively and silently.

Within our congregation, initiatives and self-help groups have been formed to deal with noise and rent problems, illnesses caused by air pollution, the crisis in the mines, problems in the workplace, living with the elderly and handicapped and the plight of our foreign fellow citizens in the area. The discovery of suffering and encouraging one another to do something about it have made people more sensitive to the suffering of strangers and willing actually to enter into it. Before we can share the suffering of others we have to know what it is to suffer ourselves. Before we can enter into the problems of strangers (close to home and far away) we must ourselves have learned not to be helpless in the face of our daily problems and to be self-confident in dealing with state authorities, business corporations and church leaders.

Perhaps this is why there has been no organized opposition to our sheltering of refugees, no slogans daubed on walls, no one leaving the church expressly on these grounds. In 1983 and 1986 our congregation offered sanctuary to Turkish families in which the breadwinner had died, so that their reason for being in Germany — the man's job — no longer existed and they were to be expelled. In both cases through church sanctuary we managed to obtain permission for the families to stay in Gelsenkirchen.

In 1983 the presbytery justified its resolution on asylum as follows:

> 1. Human beings must be treated as human beings and not as goods to be bought when they are needed and put aside as expendable (expelled) when they are no longer needed.

2. Christian congregations must always take a clear stand wherever human life is threatened and human beings are prevented from living in human dignity.

3. We recall that, in the Old Testament, strangers received special protection. In the Book of Leviticus 19:33-34 we read: "When a stranger sojourns with you in your land, you shall do him no wrong. The stranger who sojourns with you shall be to you as the native among you, and you shall love him as yourself; for you were strangers in the land of Egypt."

We recall that Jesus was driven out of his home, that he lived with the strangers of his time and laid himself open on that account to serious accusations and persecution.

We recall that Christian communities were themselves persecuted minorities for centuries and that majorities (even Christian ones) tend to exclude minorities as an uncomfortable presence.

We recall the words of Matthew 25:35ff.: "I was a stranger and you welcomed me... Then the righteous will answer him, 'Lord, when did we see thee a stranger and welcome thee?' And the King will answer them: 'Truly, I say to you, as you did it to one of the least of these my brethren, you did it to me.'"

The subjective fear of refugees

Representatives of the Amnesty International (AI) group in Gelsenkirchen asked our congregation if we could give sanctuary in the church to two men from Bangladesh who had been living in Gelsenkirchen since 1986 and had now received written notice of expulsion from the aliens office following rejection of their appeal by the courts. Ahmet Nesar and Nurul Islam, both Muslims, agreed to the suggestion of seeking sanctuary in a Christian church only because they would otherwise have been forcibly returned to Bangladesh, where they would face the threat of imprisonment, torture or death.

The presbytery advised us first to contact the Catholic and Protestant congregations in the district where the two men lived to find out whether they were willing to offer sanctuary. Only if they were not would the congregation of the Lukas Church offer sanctuary. The decisive factor prompting us to offer sanctuary in the Lukas Church was not "objectively proven" grounds for their fear of political persecution in Bangladesh, but the subjective encounter with Ahmet and Nurul as people.

Ahmet told us he had not left home, family and friends lightly or out of love of adventure, but because he had been an active member of the Bangladesh National Party (BNP). When Mohammed Ershad came to power through a military coup in March 1982, he dissolved the elected parliament and declared martial law in the country.

Of course, there were many clashes with the opposition party. The first time I was taken to prison was after a clash over a boycott of elections and the attempt to stop ballot-rigging in the constituency where I lived. When I was released I continued to work for the BNP. During an information meeting a clash developed with the Notum Bangla Party. I was able to get away, but by then I didn't dare go home because friends in the BNP were being arrested. I heard through various channels that the police were looking for me at home. My family was being threatened. My brother was pressured into paying money for them to stop looking for me. But searches were still carried out by other members of the police, so I was advised by my lawyer to leave the country.

Asylum is granted by people, not by holy places

The decision to offer sanctuary was publicly announced in a church service. Sleeping places were prepared in the church for the two Bengalis and two German helpers who would accompany them round the clock. A room was also prepared in a nearby home for young people where the two Bengalis could withdraw if they wished to be alone. During the worship service the congregation heard about the personal history of the two men, the political situation in Bangladesh and the reasons that had led them to seek asylum in the church. Members joined in building a cardboard "wall of solidarity" around the sleeping places and wrote their wishes, hopes and anxieties on it: "I wish you a home you can choose for yourselves." "The just will receive justice." "I hope you will never lose heart and that you will always believe in justice and human rights." "I hope you may always meet with people who listen to you, and who trust and help you." "Church and sanctuary. O God, I believe in you." "I hope that the death penalty may be repealed in your country so that you need not be afraid to go home. Freedom takes courage." At the close of the service we shared a Bengali meal together.

The church as a place of sanctuary is not a secret hiding place, a sanctified spot laying claim to be above the law. From the outset, immigration officials and authorities and the general public knew where the two men were staying, so that they could have intervened or taken action at any time. It is not buildings that provide sanctuary, but people. The church is not a place where the law does not apply. When the church offers sanctuary as a protest against human misuse of the law, the aim is to give those who hold political and administrative responsibility time to rethink and review their decisions. Church sanctuary does not take place outside the law, because it does not set out to oppose the law but "to preserve, complete and correct" it.

Public reactions

The news of the two men taking sanctuary in the church was reported in the regional and national media. At the same time, refugee support groups and the congregation issued open invitations to meet Ahmet and Nurul at information sessions in the Lukas Church. Meetings and discussions with the two Bengalis often took place over a shared Bengali meal in the church. Solidarity developed and grew as people met together. Many local people discovered the church as a place where people lived in the real, everyday life of the world. Especially important were the shared meals, which still take place every lunchtime and are open to everyone in the support group and anyone passing by who is interested in finding out what is going on. Several other church congregations in Gelsenkirchen have since declared that they are also willing in future to offer sanctuary.

The initial reaction of state bodies was aggressive and disapproving. The minister of justice of North Rhine-Westphalia declared: "In a state with an asylum law which is an example to the world, pastors who grant protection from expulsion procedures to asylum-seekers whose applications have been legally refused have to consider whether they are not guilty of aiding and abetting obstruction of the execution of the law." Tolerance of the continued presence of asylum-seekers whose requests had been turned down had reached its limits among the population, he said. However, criminal proceedings could not be introduced, because the sanctuary was taking place publicly and criminal law applies only if refugees are in secret hiding.

Public pressure through the media and the solidarity of Roman Catholic and Protestant congregations, district synods and the diocese of Essen then led to further conversations with the head of the city's legal department to explore the idea of submitting a new application for asylum. On humanitarian grounds, the city was prepared for the first time in its history not just to accept an appeal but to submit it as worthy of consideration to the federal office. Our lawyers suggested that this was probably the way to go, despite serious doubts, because it offered a glimmer of hope and seemed to be the only remaining option. The city representatives gave assurances that once the appeal had been submitted the two Bengalis would be free to move around in Gelsenkirchen and would receive social assistance. Even if the appeal would be turned down by the federal office, the city itself might grant permission. This would have been legally possible at any time but the city had refused, probably out of fear that it would set a precedent that could be copied by others.

Reactions in the congregation ranged from spontaneous rejection and indignation to expressions of solidarity — donations, petitions, pastoral care and joining in leisure activities with the Bengalis. Some wild rumours spread through the district: that there were 100 beds for asylum-seekers in the church; that an asylum-seeker had been lying in bed snoring during a wedding ceremony. In conversations prior to baptisms or weddings people asked anxiously whether the situation in the church would disturb their family celebration, but only one baptism was cancelled because of the sanctuary action, and the guests at one wedding added their names to the solidarity lists.

The local church as a living space

The encounter with Ahmet, Nurul and their friends from Bangladesh taught the members of our congregation and the support group to see what the social and legal situation in Germany looks like from below, from the standpoint of unknown, persecuted people. The cultural events, meals, discussions and celebrations in the church — explaining the Bengali mentality, way of life and culture — also changed the relationships of the Germans among themselves. Spontaneous meetings and displays of emotion became possible; frank conversations went on far into the night; previously buried problems and conflicts surfaced and were worked through. Age, confession and political affiliation lost their divisive power at this point: the common cause transcended generations and confessions. Catholic and Protestant Christians, non-church people and Muslims discovered something that unites them all: human suffering and protest against that suffering.

The sanctuary action strengthened our contacts with our Muslim neighbours. When the *khoja* of the district heard that the two Bengalis were having German lessons twice a week, he asked if he could join in. Later, he celebrated the Feast of Sacrifice with the Muslim Bengalis and some German friends.

Philippians 3:20 reminds us that Christians are strangers and sojourners in this world, but citizens of the future world. In the encounter between natives and refugees the natives have to free themselves of forced friendliness and the compulsive desire to offer charity and to try to make the strangers the same as themselves. It is difficult to put oneself in a stranger's place. Their different way of being, their different mentality and culture have to be respected for what they are, maintaining distance. Their "strangeness" has to be accepted in a painful process of encounter, so that we come to see these friends in a nuanced way, with all their strengths and weaknesses.

After the initial enthusiasm in the parish and in the support group — no doubt prompted in part by the fascination of the unusual (meeting with people of another culture, living and sleeping in the church) — the support group shrank considerably. It is depressing to see the changing mood of the two Bengalis, the pressure of loneliness weighing on them; and it is depressing to see how apathetic they sometimes feel. There have also been tensions among members of the support group, who draw a certain self-esteem from their commitment to the sanctuary action and feel offended when they find that there is a small group of "thinkers" conducting conversations with the authorities and politicians and a group of "workers" who organize leisure activities with the two Bengalis, work, cook and have endless conversations.

Ahmet and Nurul sometimes feel a bit like the playthings of their "helpers" if they are not included in the discussion and decision-making process. But this can only be done with the help of interpreters. The supporters sometimes wonder whether they really should try to involve the two Bengalis in every decision and whether it does not make them feel even more insecure because of the differing moods and assessments of the situation.

The Lukas congregation has become a place where Ahmet and Nurul and their Bengali friends have room to live. People are standing up for and with the two men. But what happens to the many refugees who do not manage to come in contact with a local church that is willing to grant their request for sanctuary? One of the reasons the Lukas Church congregation has given Ahmet Nesar and Nurul Islam sanctuary was precisely to encourage other congregations to do likewise to prevent more refugees being secretly deported.

CITY MISSION CENTRE, OSLO, NORWAY

Learning together with the Poor

Stig Utnem

Around 22 December Norwegians start to withdraw to their homes to prepare for their private, family-oriented celebrations of Christmas. In the "upper room" of the City Mission Centre three long tables running from the door up to the altar are spread with white cloths and candelabras. It is time for "The Great Feast" (Luke 14:15-24). Homeless people, residents of transient hostels, people struggling with drug abuse, prostitution and criminality have accepted the invitation to take part.

For more than three hours stories are told, songs are sung, including the most famous Norwegian Christmas carol *"Deilig er jorden"*, praising the beauty of God's creation, which is sung four times. "I have not sung this since I was a child," says one of the guests. During the reading of the story of the birth of Jesus Christ one could hear a pin drop.

"The Great Feast" ends with people invited to come forward to light small candles as signs of sorrow or suffering or hope or prayer. Some come in silence, some accompany their candle lighting with short speeches. The little candles remain burning as people leave the church. Two people stay up through the night to watch every one of the candles burn down.

* * *

On a Monday afternoon you can hear many different languages among the children playing in the garden of the City Mission Centre, eagerly waiting for the door to open welcoming them to the children's club. The 25 children, from 2 to 12 years old, live in the immediate neighbourhood. They come from the former Yugoslavia, Sri Lanka, Iran, Pakistan, Chile. Some of them are refugee children, newcomers to Norway, whose parents are among the few to pass through the strict Norwegian asylum legislation. Some were born in this country from parents who came in the early 1970s as migrant workers at a time when the Norwegian border was still open.

Some of the children are Hindus, some are Orthodox or Catholic Christians, most are Muslims. None belongs to the majority religion in Norway, the Lutheran confession. The activities in the children's club aim at elementary things like training them to play together and to communicate in the Norwegian language. In order to serve the neighbourhood children in this way, we have agreed with the Muslim parents not to do "religious instruction".

* * *

"He gives power to the weak" is the text written on the front wall in the church room, where people get together on Wednesday evenings for an "Everyday Mass".

We sit in a circle so that everyone can see each other, and people are invited to say their first name to the person sitting next to them. The languages used are Norwegian and English, and the Bible texts are often read in Spanish, Tamil or one of the languages of Eritrea. Many of the songs and prayers are taken from the hymnbook for the World Council of Churches' assembly in Vancouver in 1983. The people enjoy singing a Russian Orthodox *Kyrie* and an *Alleluia* from Zimbabwe. The incense that fills the room is brought to the church by Tamil refugees and comes from their Hindu tradition. The bread broken and shared during holy communion — *chappatti* or *rätti* — is baked at the Pakistani store across the street.

The people who make up the congregation at an "Everyday Mass" share the experience of feeling "homeless" in Oslo socially, culturally, spiritually or in one or the other many ways that modern people feel "far away from home" in the city. Together we sing a very simple prayer:

> Take our broken lives, O God,
> and our lone despair.
> Take us all and bring us home
> to your love and care.

* * *

During June, July and August the churches in Oslo are emptier than ever. But the ceremony of the church can be taken out into the streets.

Every Sunday evening during these three summer months, people are invited to take part in a street mass in the pedestrian area of the inner city. When the street lights come on at dusk, God kindles his light in the middle of the street. Proclamation of the good news, traditional hymns, the Lord's prayer, holy communion and the blessing — all in the middle of the business and noise of God's city.

This welcoming worship we call liturgical evangelism.

* * *

Toyenkirken, the church that houses the City Mission Centre, is located in the eastern part of Oslo's inner city, which has always been a neighbourhood of the working class, the underprivileged and the marginalized. Today immigrants, refugees, unemployed people and persons with psychiatric or drug problems live in the area or drift in and out of it.

Toyenkirken was built in 1908, and over the years the church was run by a private church organization. At its best, the church was really felt by the people in the community to be "their church". But during the 1960s and 1970s the ability of the congregation to serve the needs of the community came to a major crisis. One important reason for this was that among the first people to move out of the inner city when that became economically possible in the 1960s were the leading figures of the congregation. Since they continued to hold positions of influence in the congregation, the people who remained in the neighbourhood of the church tended to feel that they were being treated paternalistically.

The will or capacity to be challenged by the new concerns and issues of the community — the influx of immigrants or the formation of people's organizations — diminished; and in 1982 the church gave up. The City Mission of Oslo, an independent diaconal organization with more than 135 years of serving the needs of the city, asked whether it saw a way to revitalize the life and mission of Toyenkirken.

The answer they gave was this:

> There has to be a way — otherwise Christians will develop into a small and irrelevant group in the corners of the city. We will start once again searching for a simple and relevant mission together with the people in the inner city.

So the City Mission Centre was born in 1985. In seeking to revitalize the mission of Toyenkirken, a broad approach has been vital:

First, a broader view of the biblical stories and texts has been brought to life by and among poor people whose experiences of life are quite different from those of traditional churchgoers. For example, Jesus' story of the "prodigal son" (Luke 15) is taken up for discussion among people who are themselves living "in a foreign country". And what does this story say to a young woman running away from a father who has sexually abused her over ten years?

Second, as a consequence, a broader understanding of the mission of the church is necessary. For example, "dialogue with people of other faiths" in the inner city also means making the Centre hall available for Muslim weddings and Hindu youth rituals.

Third, our approach has opened up the development of human resources among people who never thought their skills or capabilities would be of any relevance or interest to the church. One example is the involvement of people with psychiatric problems in small-scale activities for which they are made co-responsible. For the first time in their adult life, they can feel useful.

For all of us, this is what is meant by people's participation in the mission of the church.

MARSEILLES, FRANCE

To Live in the World in Order to Change It

Jean-Pierre Cavalié

The *Fraternité de la Belle-de-Mai* in Marseilles, which is part of the *Mission populaire évangélique* of the French Protestant Federation, is neither a social centre nor a traditional local congregation. It grows out of a church movement which came into being in 1871 out of a desire to witness to the freedom of the gospel among the poor.

At that time the poor were the workers, and it is no accident that the choice fell first of all on workers who were organized and militant. Very early it was said that words were not enough: the challenge of the surrounding poverty also demanded action. Gradually, the three pillars which form the basis of our institution were consolidated: a church identity, a social practice, a militant approach. We have been an entirely ecumenical group for many years, simply because in the working-class context in which we are engaged there are very few Protestants. Nor is our ecumenism confined to Christians; it speaks to all men and women who need our help and whom we need to carry out our projects.

We have been established in Marseilles since 1881, first near the port, later in the northern suburbs, which are the most deprived in our "city of 100 villages". Marseilles is a city of extremes: seven inhabitants in ten have a foreign grandparent; of the 850,000 population, 106,000 live below the poverty line; in certain districts the extreme right National Front wins 45 percent of the votes. In this gateway between North and South it is difficult to separate the three major issues: the fight against unemployment and social exclusion; xenophobia and racism; and mal-development in both North and South.

In 1984-85 French society as a whole began to realize how seriously the social situation had deteriorated and discovered what was called the "new" poverty. Already in September 1982 the Catholic bishops had issued a courageous call "for new life-styles", urging simplicity and sharing to help reduce chronic unemployment. Unfortunately, what impact their call had was negative. They were asking too much. Credit cards were more popular than the Beatitudes.

The hard winter of 1984 recalled that of 1954 when the Abbé Pierre had managed to shake public apathy towards the "homeless". This time the cause of the outcast hit the headlines thanks to the famous comedian and actor Coluche. While the bishops had called for sharing, Coluche wanted immediate charitable action. But even if his campaign did not tackle the roots of the problem, it had the great merit of mobilizing public opinion and providing a direct and effective form of action through the *restaurants du coeur*, a network of canteens around France serving free meals to those in need, supported by contributions from the public.

A few months earlier, a "trade union" of the unemployed had been formed, but since it was not legally entitled to call itself that it took the name Association of Unemployed and Temporary Workers. This association was political in its approach, fighting among other things for a minimum income, but it did not have the same success in the media or in the churches as the restaurants. Soon after it gave rise to the Christian Committee for Solidarity with the Unemployed, but even today this is not widely known.

It was after Coluche's appeal that our *Fraternité* decided to offer hot meals for the homeless five days a week, in cooperation with a sister parish which provided overnight accommodation. This proved to be the starting point of our commitment to the poorest of the poor, and for us it was the beginning of a real "exodus" whose end is not yet in sight.

From the outset we wanted to get away from the simple sandwich that fills the stomach while leaving the heart outside in the street. A proper hot meal seemed a better way of demonstrating "fraternity", provided of course that we ate it together at the same table, like Christ with his disciples. How difficult we first found this physical contact with the poor — shaking hands warmly without apprehensiveness, looking one another straight in the eye without feeling superior or guilty, helping ourselves from the same dish without worrying about "catching something". It was the beginning of a conversion.

The most demanding thing of all is real *dialogue*, the exchange of words between two people. The first reaction is to seek safety in monologue — either listening without getting involved or talking nonstop to cover our embarrassment. Then there is also false dialogue — listening to the other person's "problems", feeling "sorry", trying at all costs to find a solution as though we were some kind of messiah. Surely our task is to announce the Messiah, the possibility of salvation, not to put ourselves in his place.

In 1990 we introduced two elements: organizing activities as needed from day to day, feeling for the best way forward, and regular training for the helpers. After four months we did a stock-taking with the members of the team and the visitors themselves. To our amazement, instead of asking for more coffee, card-games or wine, they asked if they could make a financial contribution to the meals and set up a "centre for the jobless".

No longer were they asking us for a helping hand, however friendly, but for an act of real solidarity. Shut up as they were in the daily reality of social exclusion and psychological loneliness, with no prospects or illusions, they were not asking us to help make their lot a little more comfortable. Instead, they were asking us to go along with them in the search for some kind of emancipation.

We were all worried. We didn't know what they were letting us in for — and neither did they. The more aware among them did know that they had to get moving. They had to stop being content to stay where they were, on the fringes of society and any human life worthy of the name. By helping them we had been soothing our own consciences without doing anything to change the situation of flagrant injustice that characterizes our society. In agreeing to set out with them on this psychological and social *exodus*, we would be obliged to put ourselves much more on a footing of equality. We realized that this exodus would transform us and convert us in one way or another. They were shifting us away from the relatively comfortable field of the "social" to the dangerous ground of the "political"; and the great majority of us did not dare to get involved in this minefield.

But a small group of us persisted. In 1985 we had chosen to receive these people; now we would at least try to take seriously their request for a centre for the jobless and study what it would imply. It then took us about a year to get acclimatized, to get used to one another and to the idea that it is possible to go further *together* — the idea of the centre for the jobless.

At present we describe ourselves as a "place of welcome and militant action". This means in practice that four afternoons a week we have workshops for various activities — theatre, painting, woodwork, cookery — and discussions on social, economic, political and spiritual questions. In theory it might seem better to help them find another job, but in fact 90 percent of the people who come to us know very well that they will never again have a steady job. So they come to us for another reason.

Work is one of the fundamental values on which our society is built. It guarantees the main part of our income and our social identity. When someone asks you who you *are*, you generally answer by saying what you *do*: I'm a plumber, a technician, a nurse. But what happens when you suddenly find yourself out of work or doing temporary jobs all the time?

Obviously, you lose much of what you *have*, in the way of income, but you also lose much of who you *are* — your social status, your friends, your self-esteem, perhaps even your object in life.

In our work with these people we are thus looking together for answers precisely at this level of being and the meaning of life. And because at the moment the future holds no prospects, we obviously find ourselves looking for alternative rules of society. Here we work in conjunction with two national organizations, the Association of Unemployed and Temporary Workers and the Christian Committee for Solidarity with the Unemployed, which militate for sharing of jobs and income.

Our solidarity makes us try to understand the underlying reasons for exclusion and unemployment. The essential cause seems to us to be political, in other words, it has to do with the rules of our society; and it is along those lines that we are looking for alternatives. In short, our solidarity towards the poor requires us to militate for a change in our society, or in the system. This is not what we had in mind when we set out, but it is where we have arrived. It is not perhaps the most comfortable position, but it is not for us to set the limits to what it means to love our neighbour.

We simply wanted to help the poor and, before we knew it, we found ourselves in the field of politics. Because of the militant side of our work and our struggle for justice through sharing, we must increasingly meet and challenge political personalities. There is no question of turning ourselves into a political party; we see ourselves rather as a kind of trade union. On the other hand, we are fully aware that if it is a case of changing policies and the way society is governed we will never succeed without the help of political parties and their representatives. The political parties are the essential tools of democracy. It is up to us to make sure that they really do serve everyone, starting with those who are poor and excluded.

The progress through these stages represents the theological and ecclesiological exodus through which we have been led by the homeless and the unemployed, French and foreign migrants, who come to us. By no means is ours the one and only way. But for us at least it has been the means of discovering that politics is the garden of neighbourly love and that there is still a lot of scrub to be cleared away.

VALLENTUNA, SWEDEN

Being Open to Refugees

Lennart Ring

During the 1970s and the early 1980s many asylum-seekers from Latin America came to Sweden. In Vallentuna, a suburb of 19,000 north of Stockholm, there were about twenty families from Chile, two from Bolivia and one from Argentina, in addition to several Iraqi families. During these years I was pastor of a Mission Covenant congregation there, with 150 members and about 450 young people enrolled in our youth work.

Shortly before Christmas 1979 the parish decided to invite a student group from Stockholm to come to our church to express their solidarity with Chile and to inform us about the situation there during a Sunday evening worship service. The programme included drama, singing and music. A few weeks earlier a group of refugees from Chile had been settled in Vallentuna. We invited them for the Sunday evening programme and they all came. Some spoke a little Swedish; none of us spoke Spanish. Some members of the Stockholm group were Chilean, but none lived in Vallentuna. During coffee after the service, a first contact was established, and the next Sunday all the Chileans came to our morning worship. Most of them met Swedish members of the congregation, who invited them to their homes. Gradually, a kind of "contact between families" programme developed.

More Latin American refugees arrived in Vallentuna. Some were relatives of those who had come earlier, but there were also others, including the Bolivians and Argentinians. All of them were asylum-seekers, which meant that they had neither a residence permit nor a work permit. The Swedish families supported them while they waited for a response to their applications, and the parish helped them to appeal if their requests were refused by the immigration authorities.

In the end, all were allowed to stay. About fifteen Chilean families came to church regularly, and for some time we had about sixty Chileans participating in Sunday services, even though the only part of the service in Spanish was the scripture lesson (read by them). Several times I asked them if they would not prefer to go to a Catholic mass or if they would like to have a visit from a Catholic priest. But the nearest Roman Catholic parish had no Spanish-speaking priest and was some distance away. It was difficult for them to go to Stockholm with their many children. "You are our priest. We want to talk to you and come to your church, if you let us," they said. "You are a real priest, aren't you?" Later I found out that my wearing a clerical collar and robe for Sunday services was the reason for their first impression that ours was a "real church" with a "real priest".

One woman asked me, "Can I pray to the Virgin Mary here in church? I know that is not what you do. But I would like to and I will do it quietly. I want to do this during the service and for myself. Can I stay with you even if I do that?" Of course I told her yes.

One Catholic family asked me to baptize their newborn son. I told them I was a Protestant and that it would not be difficult for them to see a Catholic priest and have the child baptized in a Catholic church, but they insisted. I told the story to a Catholic priest not far from our parish whom I had known for some time. "Of course, the child ought to be baptized in the Catholic church," he said, "but given the facts and future prospects, this wouldn't work out. It is with you and in your church that they live their Christian lives: you baptize him!" I did baptize him and later several other children of various families.

Whenever any of them moved to a new home, I went to bless it — not a common practice in the Protestant tradition, but usual even for non-practising Catholics. I discovered that these Latin Americans had greater expectations of me as their pastor in situations of conflict than is customary in Swedish tradition, whether the problem was within the family, between families, with Swedish neighbours or with the authorities. After a couple of years of evening classes in Spanish, it became much easier to communicate.

We did not do anything special for the Chileans in our worship or our programmes, but we made sure that they were invited, and that they understood what we wanted to communicate. They told us that this was much appreciated. They were critical of parishes and groups that organized special events for immigrants. We had close contacts with groups such as Diakonia and the Swedish Christian Youth Council, and asked them to inform us if they had any Latin American visitors whom we could invite to visit us.

Many of these people did not dare to go to any of the Roman Catholic churches where there was a Spanish-speaking priest, for fear that they might "meet people from the embassy there". In a neighbouring free church congregation of another denomination, one member was the Spanish-speaking son of a former missionary, and so-called Christian anti-communist and anti-socialist literature was given to our political refugees, which hurt them deeply.

What is proselytism? When you become a refugee, much of your life and your living conditions change. I think that in Sweden we have often been too categorical in judging immigrants, their faith and their culture. Refugees are human beings and they are all different. One must be sensitive to individuals and not ask them either to keep their former allegiance at any price or to "become Swedish" as soon as possible. Of course, we must not "recruit adherents" by taking advantage of someone else's difficult position. But a Chilean once said to me, "Why do you Swedes always put us in a special category, and why do you insist that we preserve our own old culture and adherence to our church? Do you not want us in your communities?"

There was a time when the intention of Swedish policy towards refugees was to integrate them into Swedish society at any price. I believe we have to be much more flexible. On some occasions it was necessary for the Chileans to meet on their own — for example, if something special had happened in Chile, either in the political arena or related to friends or relatives. These were the times when they wanted to meet for intercession and dialogue in church. Several of us participated together with the Chileans from Vallentuna in demonstrations in Stockholm on 11 September, the anniversary of the coup.

About the same time two Iraqi families found their way into our congregation. They were Mandaeans (followers of John the Baptist), but wanted to worship with us. After some time of being with us in worship and community they asked to become members of our parish and confess their Christian faith. They were baptized and joined the church. During these two years, the Scripture lessons were read in Arabic in addition to Swedish and Spanish.

From the very beginning, the Latin American and Iraqi women were invited to join the women's guild. When their husbands asked to be present as well, the Swedish women refused and went to get the women. Their husbands refused to let them go. But neither the Swedish nor the immigrant women gave in. There were a number of conflicts, but the men finally accepted the women's guild and its customs.

During these years the children of the Latin American families were young or in their early teens, and participated in our children's and youth work. A few of the children of the Iraqi families were teenagers. It was easy for the Iraqi girls to make friends among the teenagers of the church, but this was not the case for the boys. One of the Iraqi girls became a scout leader together with her Swedish friends. However, she was not allowed to go out after 8 p.m. This led to some problems because of leaders' meetings and overnight activities. Although her father and brothers forbade her to participate, she went anyway. The conflict increased. When some of us in the congregation helped her secretly to leave home and move elsewhere, the Iraqi men were very critical and called me to meet with them. We had many discussions and real conflicts, but finally we learned to know each other, and they began to accept that relatively grown up women could live independently in Sweden. We became friends.

The girl became a member of the congregation. Later she met an Iraqi Christian and I married them in our church. Her father and her brother said openly how much they appreciated our support and behaviour, mentioning specifically the difficulties of living in a culture which has a totally different view of relationships between men and women, children and parents. They said they understood that we had acted the way we did because we loved the girl and not because we wanted to impose our opinions and have her "become Swedish". I also conducted the weddings of two young Chilean women, both of whom married Chilean men.

It is important for a congregation to be open to refugees. A close relationship with individuals as well as with a congregation, a community which is more than a group of private people, is a real support for refugees, especially in the beginning. Here you find the kind of persistence which characterizes an institution at its best. There are churches everywhere in the world. Refugees know what to expect. In order to survive, they need more than just contacts with the authorities.

Members of the congregation and the congregation itself are enriched through the presence of people and traditions which are different from their own. And in that context it is possible to deal with conflicts related to life-style, human dignity, relationships between men and women, children and their education.

People who support refugees are often disappointed when the refugees become too self-sufficient. If demands are made, this is interpreted as a lack of gratitude.

In our congregation many older members recalled the days of the second world war, when quite a few had helped refugees from the Baltic States and from Norway who came to Sweden. They came to have a new awareness of the situation in the "third world", which was quite different from what they had heard from missionary reports or through the media.

Some of us have wondered why several persons who were regulars in congregational life now hardly ever show up. A church and a congregation can be of very real importance during one period of someone's life.

When refugees come to a new country, it is of vital importance that they be rooted in a solid community. If later they develop their own roots in Swedish society and become more independent, they do not necessarily want to stay tied to that first context.

All refugees think about going home. We talked about this among ourselves and also as Swedes and Latin Americans. Would it be difficult to return to a Catholic community in one's home country after having been involved in a Protestant congregation in Sweden? One practising Catholic who had been very active in our church returned to his country after some years in Vallentuna. When he went back to the church he had attended before, he found much alike in the two churches. Theirs was a community of believers who were close to one another; the church was near the area where he lived; and he found a place for prayer and friends with whom to celebrate and worship.

To be ecumenical in Sweden should among other things mean that in the future we ought more and more to work for the possibility for all to find *their* place within their religion and church affiliation.

BUDAPEST, HUNGARY

Forgotten Children

Tibor Missura

As a minority church comprising no more than 4 percent of the population, the Evangelical Lutheran Church in Hungary faces problems that the Roman Catholic and Reformed churches do not have. One of these is religious instruction.

During the decades of communist rule, religious teaching in public schools was given in only a few villages, and even that faced constant opposition. Most congregations decided to give their children religious instruction within the congregation itself, for example, in children's Bible study groups.

Although the pressure against the church waned somewhat in the last years of communist rule, the major upheavals of 1989 took us by surprise. As a result of this political change the church was now allowed to give religious instruction in schools, but we had neither the requisite teaching material nor staff and there was a shortage of pastors in our church.

Our own congregation in the 11th district of Budapest covers a sector with some 180,000 residents, 29 general schools, 4 secondary schools and a number of specialized schools. Our congregation has three pastors, but even with the best of intentions they cannot provide religious instruction in so many schools. Moreover, quite a number of these schools had only one or two Lutheran pupils. We therefore had to consider possible alternatives.

Before the change we had assembled some of our children within the church premises. Even that had its problems; younger children could not come alone through the bustling city traffic, and when there was no one to bring them, they stayed away. Moreover, we had arranged children's lessons at the same time as Sunday worship for the children who came to church with their parents.

After long discussion of whether we should continue this kind of programme or change our approach, we decided to bring at least the children from nearby schools to our church premises for religious instruction. This has two advantages. We can bring together children of the same age group and we can help them to feel at home in the church, so that neither the church nor the congregation will be strange to them. Meanwhile, we went to the more distant schools where there are Lutheran pupils to give them religious instruction on the spot.

One such school is attended by children from the state-run children's home whose parents are alcoholics, divorced or have otherwise neglected them. So inviting was the atmosphere our pastor was able to create in this school that children showed up for religious instruction even without being registered, including two children from the state home. Soon there were many more. The pastor was glad to receive them; and when she made contact with the home authorities, who were ultimately responsible for them, the director readily gave permission for the children to attend the religious instruction classes.

A month later the director asked the pastor to help organize a Christmas programme for the home, noting that most of the children had no other place to spend Christmas. This enabled the pastor to meet even more children and grow fond of them. After Christmas the director asked the pastor to organize religious instruction at the home itself. The children were free in the afternoons after they had finished the day's classes and their assignments. The pastor was happy to oblige, as that gave her the opportunity to devote more pastoral attention to the children.

So it happened that the socially disadvantaged children in this state-run home were able to get to know the Christian faith. As more and more children became involved, they eventually had to be divided into three groups. The pastor asked older pupils from her religious study class to serve as assistants, thus giving them an unexpected introduction to actual religious practise. The enthusiastic response of the children was a further incentive for even greater personal involvement.

Many of the children in the home had not been baptized; and those who expressed a wish to be were prepared for baptism at the end of the school year. The central concern of the pastor and her assistants was to make these forgotten children feel that God cared, and baptism could be a special sign of that. When fourteen of the candidates for baptism asked to have a common baptismal ceremony, the question arose as to who would be their godparents, since only a few had a relative available. At that stage the congregation was brought into the picture. They were told about this special involvement of the pastor and her young helpers and so, along with some of the educators, enough parishioners gladly volunteered as godparents. Godparents-to-be and children met several times before the ceremony. They went on excursions together or the children spent weekends with their godparents and family and so got to know each other. Thus many children found a "home".

The baptism itself was incorporated into the congregation's Sunday worship. There was an exceptionally large turnout, with many coming from the children's home. For children and adults alike, the baptismal service and the agape meal that followed were a special manifestation of how the love of our Saviour surpasses parish boundaries, our Saviour who loves the children above all: "Let the little children come to me, and do not stop them, for it is to such as these that the kingdom of God belongs."

7. Opening up Worship

My house shall be called a house of prayer for all peoples (Isa. 56:7).

If, therefore, the whole church comes together and all speak in tongues, and outsiders or unbelievers enter, will they not say that you are out of your mind? But if all prophesy, an unbeliever or outsider who enters is reproved by all and called to account by all (1 Cor. 14:23-24).

Worship is the heart of the life of a Christian community. But this heart should beat for all.

- How accessible are our worship services?
- How far can a visitor experience that he or she is being addressed, is being included?

Local congregations have tried in many ways to open up their worship services to the whole community, for example, by sharing even the preparation of services with "outsiders", by celebrating festive services in the open air, by widening the range of participation, even by changing the architecture of their place of worship.

- Who is responsible for the worship life in your congregation — the pastor/priest? Anyone else?
- What opportunity do "ordinary believers" or even "outsiders" have to participate in the preparation and performance of worship services?
- How does the worship relate to the culture of the people?

Building Bridges through Worship

Tony Gulbrandzen

The parish of Tumba, in the suburbs of Stockholm, has about 20,000 inhabitants, of whom about 17,000 belong to the Church of Sweden. Several years ago a report by the Institute for Religious Sociology disclosed that our parish had the lowest percentage of attendance at worship services in all of Sweden. As one newspaper put it, Tumba was the most secularized parish in the most secularized country in Europe.

An average of 80 people attended our two parish churches, and that number was gradually decreasing every year. These statistics obviously stirred up all of us on the parish team: priests, musicians, deacons, parish workers, and the members of the parish council. What were we to do in order for Christian faith and life to continue to be a living reality in the parish of Tumba?

We decided to begin work on our worship life in different ways. First, we asked those who came to church to bring their neighbours and friends some Sunday. One who did told us in no uncertain terms: "Never again will I bring a friend to church. It was terrible! Worship was dull, the hymns were sad, the sermon was incomprehensible, there was no life at all. In fact I was ashamed to have to admit to my friend that worship could be like that."

We concluded that we had to work at the liturgy — the proclamation of the word and the content of our worship — if we wanted to speak to people of our time. This meant not just hunting for more people, but recognizing that the quality of what we do in worship is extremely important. Worship has to mean something to those participating in it, and it must be related to their faith as well as to their daily life. Our aim was to root the content of our worship deeply in the Bible and in the world of faith. It should be open, so that a newcomer to the context would feel welcome, and take up questions that concern the people around us.

We realized that it would be impossible for priests, musicians and deacons to cope with all of this on their own. We had to involve more people in order to be close to the thinking, reflections and needs of the people of our parish. We therefore decided to start by working step by step.

Step 1

Many different groups in our parish meet in the church facilities —
Bible study groups, choirs, youth groups, confirmands, parents'
groups. Each of these groups was given responsibility for two Sundays
in the autumn and two in the spring. It was their task to meet with the
priest, deacon and organist to prepare "their" service. They would
discuss the Bible texts with the pastor who was to preach, make
suggestions for the hymns and songs to be sung and work on the
prayers and intercessions. They also helped with different aspects of
the service: greeting those who came to church, carrying the cross and
candle in the procession, reading the text and the prayers. After the
service they hosted the coffee hour and arranged discussion groups for
those present.

This meant more commitment and livelier worship, and "our own"
people began to come to church more frequently.

Step 2

At this point we wondered how to reach those who are nominal
members of our church but who do not care at all about us and our
services.

We learned from research in sociology of religion that those who go to
church do so for a specific reason — because a child sings in the choir or
is preparing for confirmation or because a person's organization is in
charge this Sunday. We realized it was important to create such
"reasons".

We began by writing a letter to all the organizations in our area: the
Red Cross, Save the Children, clubs for retired people, political associations, organizations for the disabled, sports clubs — any organizations in
which we could find a contact person. Many of them were interested in
the idea of a "Church Sunday", and we now have one almost every other
week throughout the year, planned by some organization.

Representatives of the organization attend our preparatory meeting
for the service. They tell us what hymns they would like to sing, offer
their insights into the biblical texts and suggest what should be prayed
for in the intercessions. They are also welcome to read the texts on
Sunday, to pray and sing. During the coffee hour they can make a
presentation about their organization and its activities. The parish in turn
uses their address list to notify their members that their organization will
be in charge of the service on the next Sunday and invite them
personally to be present.

Obviously this has had an effect not only on the Sunday services, but also on the image of the church in the local community. When the local association for the protection of nature visited us, we were informed about specific environmental problems in the region. Intercessions dealt with these problems. After the service, with the leaders of the association, we visited a unique environmental area nearby which is at risk.

When the second largest business in the area, a paper mill, visited us, we got into a detailed discussion among ordinary church people, trade union members and company officials on human dignity and work. When a fatal accident occurred there some time later, we were immediately contacted for help.

Together with Amnesty International and its local branch we organized a service on the theme of suffering and persecution, with hymns, songs, prayers and sermon centred on this topic.

Step 2 caused a real change in the content of our worship services. The people of the church have become more conscious of the problems of our society and our environment. People at the local level have understood in different ways that the parish cares about questions which are common to all. It has also meant that in four years attendance at our services has increased by forty percent.

Step 3

The third step of our project involved organizing "Church Sundays" for our different institutions: homes for the elderly, community service centres, schools, homes for the disabled. We also plan to invite different housing areas to their "Church Sunday". It is our plan that every Sunday some group will have this opportunity to be responsible.

We were concerned that our invitations would be accepted once but not again. This has certainly been true in some cases, but not for all. Some come again, and the nucleus of the parish has increased. By now we have moved beyond Step 1, so that all can take part in the shaping and developing of worship. Instead of our original approach, we ask all those who want to participate to become part of one of four large preparatory groups. Each is responsible for one Sunday a month and does all the basic planning. Representatives of organizations still participate actively. All members of organizations who wish to be involved are offered the possibility of working in one of these four groups. And some of them respond from time to time to that offer.

We feel there is more commitment to worship and many more participate. This is important to us.

AKADEMGORODOK, SIBERIA, RUSSIA
A Family United by the Sacraments
Boris Pivowarow

For almost a thousand years it was impossible to imagine a settlement in Russia without a church. Every undertaking would begin with a blessing — whether it was thanksgiving before ploughing or sprinkling the oven with holy water before baking bread. Then, over the last seven decades, words like "thanksgiving", "consecration", "blessing" were almost erased from our vocabulary. Our own city of Akademgorodok had never heard the ringing of church bells, had never seen church domes. Akademgorodok is located in the suburban area of Novosibirsk, the largest city in Siberia. With over 20 research institutes and one of the best Russian universities, Akademgorodok possesses a tremendous intellectual potential.

In December 1989 an Orthodox parish dedicated to All Saints Glorifying the Russian Land was organized here. The first divine liturgy took place in June 1990, on Trinity Day, Russia's beloved holiday. The service was held outdoors in a church whose walls were birch trees and whose cupola was the sky itself. Over 300 people, some kneeling, stayed for several hours under a steady rain.

Even before a new wooden church was completed in 1991, the faithful in Akademgorodok led an active parish life, celebrating all the church feasts. The Blessing of Water on the day of the Baptism of our Lord took place outdoors with the temperature below -20. By the end of the service the water in the font was covered with ice, but none of the many who came to take some holy water left empty-handed. The first Easter was also celebrated in the open, with festive refreshments laid on the logs and blessed Easter cakes and eggs shared on the spot, a new beginning for future common meals.

Now we have built a small wooden church with a belfry and seven silvery domes and a small wooden hut nearby for the Sunday school. The number of parishioners coming to our services continues to grow, and several thousand people have already been baptized. Following the traditions of mercy and charitable works in Russia, a sisterhood of nurses was created in the name of the martyred Grand Duchess Elizabeth Feodorovna. They take care of sick and needy people through a "Hospital at Home" service, consultative medical help for parishioners and children, nursing the patients in the trauma unit and the cardiological unit of the hospital. The parish also operates a retirement home near Akademgorodok.

The parish gives special attention to children's education. It has developed a project for a Siberian Religious Centre with the main task of acquiring and sharing its experience in diakonia and continuing church education. A basic element in church education is the parish Sunday school, which is attended by nearly 200 children of all age groups.

In 1992 the church opened a parochial school, the St Sergius of Radonezh Orthodox Gymnasium. In summer the students of the gymnasium and Sunday school can vacation at the Orthodox camp together with their parents.

The future of our country depends greatly on the forces which influence the education of the young generation. The basic task of the gymnasium is to combine the Orthodox education of the children with science teaching of the highest standards. This is possible because many of the teachers at the gymnasium are also professors and instructors at the university or researchers from the local scientific institutes.

While understanding the scientific method of perceiving the world, our instructors also recognize its limits. Science does not become an all-powerful idol but takes its appropriate place in a pupil's life, regardless of his or her future profession. All the instructors are parishioners of our church. Together with the children they attend services, perform the sacrament of confession, receive holy communion and sing in the choir. This creates an atmosphere of spiritual proximity and a common world-view between the instructors and the pupils.

Memorable concerts have been organized by the pupils for the local community on Christmas, Easter and the day of Slavonic culture. These presentations acquaint people with important events in Christian and national history. There are many interesting personalities in the gymnasium and the parish. Outstanding scholars give lectures to the children and together with the professional artists and musicians help children to master the spiritual, musical and artistic traditions.

The parish lives the life of a large family united by the sacraments of the church. They share both the joy of celebrations, common meals, baptisms and weddings and the sorrow of funerals, commemoration repasts and requiems. The missionary and apostolic vocation lies in the very nature of the church. Often children introduce their parents to our church in the desire to share with loved ones their own newly found feeling of love for the Lord, and many of these parents are among the most active members of the parish.

It is in bringing people together in this way that the mission of the church lies. In the church all are equal before God regardless of education or social status; it is only in the church that a person comes to realize that he or she is free of all systems and ideologies, that all his or her deeds are transient, that his or her spirit is not only that of human beings but also that of the Holy Spirit. Listening to the word of God and accepting it, the Christian becomes a missionary, an agent of the eternal divine Logos who says quietly, "Come to me, all you that are weary and I will give you rest" — and peace comes down on you, and with peace in your soul you always do what is good.

SOUTHOWRAM, ENGLAND

God's Fair

Richard Golding

The parish of Southowram is basically an extended village community situated on a hilltop in West Yorkshire, England. The population of the parish is around 3000. The nearest towns — Halifax and Brighouse — suffered much from the decline of the textile and machine tool industries, but are now showing encouraging signs of re-orientation and growth. The principal industry in Southowram itself is stone-quarrying. Otherwise it remains a residential and semi-rural area.

There are three fairly distinct groups of residents. First, there are those who spring from Southowram families, the "villagers". Most are elderly people who remember the village before its post-war expansion, and are mainly artisans. This group is well-represented within the church and tends to be rather conservative.

Second, there has been a sizeable middle-class population since some smart housing developments were built in the village. This group includes professionals, self-employed persons, managers and supervisors. They, too, are influential within the church and are, with some exceptions, rather conservative and distrustful of "enthusiasm".

A third group has come into Southowram as a result of the development of three council housing estates. These persons have unskilled or semi-skilled occupations and live in relative poverty. Many are now unemployed, and there is quite a number of single-parent families. Because of the activities of a minority of these people (particularly teenagers), the whole group tends to be regarded with suspicion and indeed fear by the others. Most of these people are on the fringe of church life, if present at all.

Average Sunday morning attendance at the Anglican parish church of St Anne's numbers about eighty adult communicants. We have a fair spread of people between the ages of 30 and 70, but we are rather weak in the late teens and early twenties. In liturgy and outlook St Anne's stands firmly in the Anglo-Catholic tradition within the Church of England. The only other denomination represented in the parish are the Methodists, whose chapel has a small and ageing congregation. Southowram is part of a very large Roman Catholic parish, and the nearest Catholic church is in Halifax.

It had been recognized for some time at St Anne's that we needed to give a higher priority to evangelism. An impulse to action came in 1991 with the "God Cares" mission to Calderdale. There was a powerful sense of God's presence with us and an eager expectation of great things to come as more than a hundred local churches of all denominations came together to proclaim the gospel in new and exciting ways. We were joined for the fortnight of the mission by a team of student missioners from Oxford.

The parish council formed a working party of seven (it later grew to twelve) to plan our response to the mission. We prayed for the guidance and strength of the Holy Spirit and were soon totally astonished by what it seemed we were being asked to do. A mere twelve weeks later, on 15 September, we staged "God's Fair" in co-operation with the Methodist chapel.

"God's Fair" was a twelve-hour open-air festival of Christian music and entertainment without any denominational label. Our aim was that the people should be able to come and enjoy themselves and, we hoped, encounter Christ in a non-threatening environment. So that no one need be excluded, admission was free. The event consisted of non-stop Christian rock music from professional and amateur bands on two specially constructed stages in a field. Around the stages, arranged in tents and marquees like a fair, were catering facilities, displays by Christian groups, a Christian book and record stall and a balloon race to carry the message far and wide. There was choral and organ music, children's entertainment and Christian drama at the church and church hall.

The centrepiece of the day was an open-air service with an evangelistic preacher, in which we sought to re-enact symbolically the feeding of the five thousand using five enormous loaves of bread and two huge "fish". The day ended with a mammoth bonfire and fireworks, accompanied by the singing of some lively worship songs.

The logistics of staging such a first attempt at organized evangelism in twelve weeks from start to finish were somewhat daunting. However, God was present with us in power and everything that was needed was provided. The little organizing team often felt more like privileged spectators than organizers. For those involved, "God's Fair" was one long miracle, exhilarating and profoundly faith-deepening. Our lives will never be the same again!

"God's Fair" touched other lives as well. Around 2000 people — many of them not affiliated with a church — attended the event. No one underwent a dramatic conversion then and there, but we have seen in our own parish and heard from others how "God's Fair" was a turning-point for many on their journey to — or back to — God. It seemed to develop into more a mission *to* the churches than a mission *by* the churches; and I am convinced that the seeds planted that day will mature and grow in God's own time. "God's Fair" did catapult the two churches in Southowram onto centre stage in the village and made us a talking point. The people of Southowram were left in no doubt that there are Christians among them and that God means business in this place.

After so many blessings it was inconceivable that we should allow the matter to rest there; and we set out to re-organize our Sunday evening service. On three Sundays a month we now hold an informal service as a form of outreach in the local community centre, in local pubs and in a centre for the elderly in a nearby housing complex.

In the wake of "God's Fair", one member of the committee suggested that we organize a mini-mission centred on baptism, contacting those in the village who had not been baptized and offering them the grace of the sacrament. We were particularly concerned to reach adults, but were also eager for parents to present their children for baptism. A very carefully planned campaign began in April 1992 and culminated in an open-air service on Pentecost Sunday in the centre of the village, followed by an evening confirmation service with a party afterwards.

"Sunrise Southowram", as the campaign was known, involved a questionnaire distributed to every home in the village, mailings explaining what was going on and a little about baptism, a poster campaign and occasional "spectacles" such as marching through the village to the site of the service with a large wooden cross to plant in the field to claim the ground for Jesus Christ. As part of the campaign we filmed, edited and produced our own video, exploring evangelism through a different medium. The video depicts the journey to God through baptism by means of pictures, images and music and a minimum of words.

At the worship service, conducted by the Anglican and Roman Catholic priests and the Methodist minister, two hundred people, many of whom were not practising Christians, renewed their baptismal vows together. In the weeks preceding the service, six adults were baptized in church and more have come forward since. Moreover, at the evening confirmation service twelve adults were confirmed — an enormous number for us.

During and after the "Sunrise Southowram" campaign we were obliged to confront some uncomfortable realities. Already in the planning stages of "Sunrise" it became clear that most of the Methodist congregation had little or no enthusiasm for the project, and they largely dropped out. Moreover, it was evident that we were failing to carry our own congregation with us. Attendance by members of the congregations at the outreach services had remained low. The impact of the questionnaire was limited by the fact that only members of the organizing team were prepared actually to talk to people as the questionnaires were returned. And we had only one volunteer to host a coffee and video evening for friends and neighbours. Everyone was thoroughly impressed with the video, but no one seemed prepared to use it as a means of sharing their faith with those around them.

We were running ahead too far, too fast. It must be said that there had already been a considerable backlash in some quarters of the congregation against "God's Fair" — which we in our enthusiasm had largely ignored. While a growing number of people in the congregation were becoming enthusiastic about mission, the majority were not. Dangerous and damaging tensions began to appear. The group which had organized "God's Fair" and "Sunrise Southowram" began to be seen as a clique — and a lack of communication on both sides did little to ease this. It was time for rethinking.

For the following year, the programme centred on drawing the congregation together, fitting the church to receive more new Christians and preparing members of the congregation to play their part, whatever it may be, in active evangelism in a supportive environment. The aims were to widen the outreach committee and to communicate its activities more effectively. A programme of events was organized within the church to create a deeper sense of community, while a programme of prayer and teaching in church and in smaller groups would allow the Holy Spirit to lead us all more deeply into a life of Christian discipleship and witness.

HELSINKI, FINLAND

The Thomas Mass

Klaus Kasch

The Thomas Mass is a service for the "Thomases" in our secularized society — people who find the normal language of Christian liturgy off-putting, who see the church as a closed society, the doubters and the sceptics on the fringes of the church and those who feel they no longer have a place in it.

Every Sunday evening at 6:00 p.m., except in the months of June, July and August, as many as 1200 people gather in the Agricola Church in Helsinki. The service lasts from two to two-and-a-half hours. Forty to fifty people are involved in the leadership of each service, with many of the main duties carried out by lay people.

I met the people who started the project on a study trip to Scandinavia. Later a small group of us went to Helsinki to study the phenomenon more closely.

The form of the service

When we arrived at the church at 5:30, the choir and band were still practising. The atmosphere was noisy and relaxed. Gradually the church began to fill up, with all kinds of people coming in ones and twos or in small groups. The majority were women, but there were also quite a few men; many were young people in the 18-30 age-bracket, still more of the middle generation and a few old people. They greeted one another, chatted briefly, then sat quietly and prepared themselves for worship.

The service begins with a procession of the celebrants carrying the icon of the cross and lighted candles while the choir leads the congregation in singing *Laudate omnes gentes* in Latin and Finnish. One member of the team is responsible for each service. On this particular Sunday it was Reijo Telaranta, who greeted the congregation, called them to worship and welcomed two sets of visitors — our group and a large group of Swedish guests. He mentioned that it was the birthday of a woman in our group; there was applause and the choir led the congregation in singing "happy birthday". All heads turned to give a friendly greeting to the foreigners, who were easy to recognize from the headphones they wore for interpretation. In this packed church, with people standing at the back, the fifty foreigners were no problem. They were simply accepted into the fellowship of people preparing to worship. *Oculi nostri ad dominum Jesus*, the congregation sang, and I could easily join in Latin and Finnish.

"In the name of the Father, the Son and the Holy Spirit" — this is how the service begins. Then Olli Valtonen told us that he and his wife were expecting visitors and she had asked him to help to clean the house. He didn't feel like it, he said, and it was hard work; but with every trash bag he carried out, the easier it got, the tidier the house looked and the better he felt. We are like that house, he went on. In us, too, dirt and disorder accumulate over time, and all the things that pile up detract from the joy and carefreeness of life. We also need a "spring cleaning" every now and then — and that was what we would now do, in confession.

With that he turned to the altar, and a man and a woman came forward and knelt beside him. With pauses for short moments of silence and a *kyrie eleison* sung by the choir and congregation, each made a short prayer of confession — very personal, but not intimate or embarrassing. It was easy to share in these confessions, the silence and the responses. Then all three turned to face the congregation and after a short pause there followed the ancient yet eternally new formula: "In the power which the Lord has given his church, I grant you absolution and remission of all your sins, in the name of the Father, the Son and the Holy Spirit. Amen."

Following an anthem by the choir came a time of intercessions. Several side-altars are set up to receive the different prayer requests for victims of highway accidents and their families, for the unemployed and people plunged into poverty by Finland's economic crisis, for the environment, for justice in the world. On each altar was a candle to light, an icon and a small basket in which anyone could place a piece of paper with a prayer concern. On one altar a paper in a child's scrawl asked us to pray for parents to stop quarrelling and not to separate; another mentioned the problems of drug addiction. For 20 minutes the choir sang while the people moved around the church to the different altars to present their prayers or went forward to the altar to be anointed or blessed. Then came a general prayer of intercession during which some prayers were read out and underlined by the singing of a *kyrie*.

The prayer section of the service was followed by the proclamation of the word. Scripture readings, sermon and confession of faith were set in a framework of anthems and songs led by the choir and accompanied by the band or the synthesizer. This part of the service focussed on the last story in the gospel of John, in which Jesus asks Peter three times: "Do you love me?" Standing on the altar steps and speaking without notes, the preacher described an elderly couple sitting at the breakfast table, the husband buried in his newspaper, the wife busy with her own thoughts until suddenly she asks, "Tell me, do you love me?" From behind his newspaper he remarks that he told her he did thirty years ago, but she insists and asks a second time, "Do you love me?" And as he tells her that he does, he sits there behind his newspaper wondering what he can possibly have done wrong in the past few days. When she repeats the question a third time, he is forced to put down his newspaper and come to grips with this challenge.

The preacher explained that Jesus is asking us too: Do you love me? What do we know about this Jesus? What kind of history do we have with him and he with us? Do we leave room for him in our lives? The impact of the address was direct. The preacher kept a tight grip on his listeners' attention, guiding their thoughts but not trying to convert them or lead them to a specific goal. After all, the story in John 21 is not about Peter's love, but about the forgiving love of Christ for Peter. So on this Sunday after Easter the preacher wanted to show the congregation that Christ's love makes new beginnings possible for all of us. Saying yes to him now does not mean a burdensome commitment for all time to come but the grace that enables us to let yesterday be and strike out for new horizons — which may not be as new as all that, for we remain ourselves. But the chance to make a fresh start exists just the same — again and again.

The communion part of the service used ancient Orthodox music and formulas which are very solemn yet at the same time warm-hearted. Absolution after confession and the institution of the Lord's Supper are the only parts of the service reserved to the clergy; every other part can also be conducted by lay people. Communion is served at six different points in the church with the people coming forward to receive it. In each case a pastor and a lay person hand the bread and wine to them. After a prayer of thanksgiving and the blessing, the crowd of celebrants processes out of the church with the icon of the cross while the congregation sings the final hymn.

After the service everyone is invited down to the church's spacious crypt for a time of fellowship over a cup of tea. Here again several hundred people take up the invitation and spend a moment together on Sunday evening.

How the services came about

The service that Sunday evening was moving, but difficult to classify. In some respects it was reminiscent of a charismatic service — anointing, blessing, the nature of many of the songs. But some very ancient liturgical traditions of the Orthodox church were also unmistakably present. That in itself, however, does not explain why people regularly come in such numbers to these services. I believe there is something else that makes these services different, and it has to do with the way in which they came about.

In the autumn of 1987, Olli Valtonen, a theologian working as an editor with a daily newspaper, and Mikea Ruokanen, a professor of theology at the university, got together to think about new ways of carrying out evangelism in the city. What seemed most urgently needed was a church service that would also appeal to their friends and colleagues outside the church — as one member of our group put it, a service they wouldn't need to be ashamed of. In other words, *a service for the Thomases, for the modern individuals who always also have doubts: a service for the Thomas in ourselves.*

They began by writing to their friends, lay and clergy, inviting them to think about the possibilities for such a service. A group of 15 people which came together gradually grew to 40. For a while they divided themselves into different sub-groups working on various aspects: silence and meditation, singing and music, liturgy, organization. Initially they had no intention of holding another additional service of their own but simply wanted to think about possible ways of altering existing services. But after six months of discussion and theoretical work they chose the Agricola Church and fixed a date — April 10, 1988 — for the first Thomas Mass.

This course of action seems to have been a success. They have found the right formula to respond to the spiritual state and needs of many people, in particular of many who have not previously been churchgoers. What the originators of the Thomas Mass wanted to do was to make something of the mystery of the faith and of God's holiness and love accessible to modern secular individuals. The guiding theme of these services is the rediscovery of the transcendental in modern society.

And to judge from the faces of the worshippers they have largely succeeded.

Organization

A special association, open to anyone, has been formed. Its committee is chiefly concerned with financial matters — the use of the offerings collected, the cost of musical instruments and sound systems, hymn books, etc. In addition there is a leadership group which meets every Thursday morning to discuss topical issues, review the previous Sunday's service and prepare the two coming ones. The member of the leadership team responsible for leading a Sunday service puts together the team to lead it, including a choirmaster and enough people from the long list of volunteers to help with the many large and small duties involved.

A council of 85 elders, elected for one year, is responsible for all the activities that have developed around the Thomas Mass — for instance, prayer groups during the week to take up the prayer requests placed in the baskets during the service, theological and liturgical instruction for those taking part and courses of instruction in the faith for any who are interested. The council of elders also ensures that people who come looking for help and express their worries at the service are directed to a source from which they can receive support. The council of elders may also take up new initiatives, but the principle is that before anything can be offered there have to be people ready to offer it. They do not attempt to react to every need but only to what is within the means at their disposal.

The Thomas Mass has become a permanent feature within the Evangelical Lutheran Church of Finland. The bishops have agreed to this worship experiment and "ordain" those who serve communion. It has become clear from sociological research that the Thomas Mass does not compete with other church services or events. Initial fears that it might do so were quickly dissipated. Every week about one-quarter of the people attending the Thomas Mass are there for the first time, and the great majority of them have had little or nothing to do with the church until then. Fifty percent of the worshippers attend the service more or less regularly, and many of them have likewise had no previous church connection. Others already were or still are active in their own congregations.

Is this developing into a "church within the church"? As far as the association and its members are concerned this is certainly the case. Yet the service is made so open and inviting, and has such relatively uncomplicated links with rest of the Lutheran national church that it does not create a problem. The people who have gathered here are not a group of particularly devout Christians who consider themselves different from others, but rather a group of Christians celebrating worship with one another and for others in a special way.

BROMLEY-BY-BOW, LONDON, ENGLAND

Faith Is about Imagination

Donald Elliott

In 1985 the Bromley-by-Bow congregation of the United Reformed Church had a loyal congregation of ten elderly persons. The building had strong wire mesh around the grubby windows to defend it against vandalism. Its situation in Bruce Road in London's East End meant that its neighbourhood is one of long-term social deprivation in high-density post-war housing. There are also some remnants of Victorian dwellings and, significantly, an artistic community. The huge London Docklands development nearby is also having an impact on the area, with some younger professional people moving in.

The conversion of this congregation from embattled survivor to neighbourhood resource has come as a result of the decision of the congregation to address an open-ended call to a minister committed to the exercise of imagination. In fact, says Andrew Mawson, "faith is about imagination". Step by step, the congregation has made decisions about opening up and transforming their buildings for a variety of uses, all designed to encourage local people to exercise their imagination.

First it was the needs of local artists to have space to do their sculpture and painting. Then it was for a group of differently abled people to meet. Later there were the needs of pre-school children and their working mothers. Then there was food.

At the heart of all this business, in every sense, is the actual church. A simple altar, surrounded by wooden pews and canopied by a curious sort of suspended tent, is at the eucharistic centre of this project.

"Denomination is unimportant here," says Mawson. What is important are personal relationships and the building of a community. The way these are fostered is through creativity and artistic endeavour. Church-going is not necessarily a part of that. If they come, they come; if not, they carve wood, or design mosaics, plant the garden or meet friends to share food at the Pie in the Sky café.

Drawing on the vast artistic heritage of the East End of London (the four to five thousand artists in the area probably make it the second largest artistic community in the world after Manhattan), the Church Centre has made a fundamental commitment to exploring the connections between art and theology, between creativity and belief. A leading figure is Santiago Bell, a Chilean refugee and director of the workshops at the Centre.

Bell believes passionately in the necessity of art in the community. A one-time fellow of the pioneering educationalist Paolo Freire, and now in exile following years of persecution and torture, he works full-time at the Centre as well as exhibiting his often disturbing wood sculptures both here and abroad. "We are living and working on the Monday after the seven days of creation," he says.

A number of the crafts pursued in the workshops are often classified as "dying": stone masonry, wood-carving, stained-glass work. But this is not the case here. All around are examples of work being done. The stairs leading to the "quiet room", where pastoral interviews and counselling take place, are made entirely of wood by a team of women joiners, who also fitted out the brick-floored kitchen for the café, staffed by local members of the community six days a week. Inside the quiet room, the single window is of beautiful orange and red stained glass made on site, a craftswoman's interpretation of the resurrection.

The worshipping congregation remains small (about 25 regulars). Direct evangelism is not done. The design of the church is a theological statement of the whole project, whose aim is to be holistic, challenging both social structures and individuals. The symbols of the eucharist are central. The commitment is to share life with all people, recognizing that the new historical situation requires the church seriously to review its mission. This urgent theologizing is done in the concrete context, since concern for the poor in East London is a complex matter, and it is not possible to transplant models developed in the Two-Thirds World.

The worship space is surrounded by the children's nursery, rather like the medieval cathedral in the city marketplace, the cosmic drama in the midst of the mundane. If it is true that "we are the environments we live in", then there must be a considerable spiritual influence on the 600 people per week who pass through.

The liturgical space is no longer wired and shuttered off from the street. Plate glass means that everything is visible from outside. The surrounding children's play area points to the significance of children to the gospel.

The liturgy itself embodies a broad ecumenical understanding, taking what are seen to be the most helpful aspects of the historic Christian tradition to create something in which children, adults and strangers can take part. There is midweek prayer, recognizing that the traditional rhythm of regular Sunday worship no longer holds in this community.

Because of the close relationship with the neighbourhood, many have shared in the liturgy and even composed their own liturgies (some of astounding beauty and understanding). The result is that the church's liturgical life is no longer a compartment separate from the whole life of the community. Simplistic divisions and institutional categories are resisted.

The Centre is now involved in major local development projects. They are developing a three-acre derelict park behind their buildings which will incorporate a health centre in the form of a cloister, as well as a café, open workshops and a performance area. A European project has also begun, since the Channel tunnel Rail-Link will emerge about a kilometre from the Centre. This project has grown out of the Centre's participation in a three-year European Conference on Citizenship involving France, Germany and the UK, which has culminated in an exchange of nursery workers between the Centre and Nancy, France.

8. Building Common Witness

There is one body and one Spirit, just as you were called to the one hope of your calling: one Lord, one faith, one baptism, one God and Father of all, who is above all and through all and in all (Eph. 4:4-6).

Europe is the continent where the Christian church got divided — first between East and West, Rome and Byzantium, later within the Western church between Rome and Wittenberg, Canterbury and Geneva. And these divisions gave rise to more divisions later.

Thank God we see divided churches today trying to overcome their divisions and committing themselves to common witness.

In many places congregations of different confessional affiliation are neighbours. The very fact of different churches at one place proclaiming the one and the same Christ yet often competing with each other is a scandal. There are signs of hope, signs of a new beginning in ecumenical fellowship where local congregations of different confessions begin to do together what they can without violating their consciences. Some would like to go further, but there are problems which cannot be solved on the local level.

- What Christian communities of other churches exist in your area?
- How far do you know them?
- What are the relations between your congregation and these others?

MEYRIN-CITÉ, GENEVA, SWITZERLAND

Two Congregations under One Roof

Philippe Bonte

In Meyrin-Cité, the Catholics and the Protestants have the keys to each other's facilities. This is a striking symbol of a real-life ecumenical experience.

Meyrin-Cité is a large housing development near Geneva's international airport, built at the beginning of the 1960s. Over the years more apartment blocks have been added, so that now the town has some 22,000 inhabitants. In the most recent census more than 110 nationalities were counted. In the middle of the apartment blocks is a huge car-park and two centres — a shopping plaza and the Ecumenical Centre shared by the Roman Catholic and Protestant churches.

At the outset the Christian communities in Meyrin-Cité met in two small temporary wooden chapels. In late 1969 an opinion poll organized by the Catholic and Protestant parish councils showed that a considerable majority of parishioners of both confessions, who included many young couples, were in favour of building two churches under the same roof, responding to the wish for closer relations and Christian unity while reducing construction costs.

Work began in July 1974; the symbolic cornerstone was laid in a common celebration in September. The work was completed in late autumn 1975, and the two communities officially took possession of their new premises at an ecumenical watch-night service at Christmas that year. That service was a challenge in itself, both for the Catholics, who are fond of their traditional midnight mass, and for the Protestants, who are not in the habit of holding a midnight service at Christmas. The inauguration service took place on 8 May 1976.

The building and its management

The building comprises two main levels. On the upper ground floor is a large central foyer with places of worship on either side: a Catholic church with 300 seats and a Protestant chapel with 100 seats. Each can be completely opened up onto the central hall, creating a single attractive room for larger gatherings. The lower ground floor contains a large multi-purpose room, six meeting rooms and a small hall with a fully-equipped kitchen.

Each church owns part of these premises and grounds and carries out its own parish activities in the premises that belong to it. But the two communities also have common activities, promoted by a joint congregational committee, which also manages the building. Each parish council appoints an equal number of members to the joint congregational committee, and the chair alternates annually between the two communities. One of its main tasks is "constantly bringing before the two communities the deeper questions concerning their existence, and helping to stimulate reflection", as well as "acting as a link between the congregational bodies in a regular dialogue".

Activities

Ecumenism in Meyrin is not just an appendix to the various other activities of the Catholic and Protestant communities; it constitutes a central element in many of our activities: occasions when we *do* something together, when we *experience* something together and when we *reflect* together to deepen our relations.

Our first "activity" together was an ecumenical fair, which has now become a tradition, bringing together an impressive number of people every year and making an important financial contribution to the maintenance of the Centre.

Other activities undertaken together have included help in caring for asylum-seekers (especially in 1988-89), organization of a stand during the "Third World Week" organized by the local district authorities every four years, a bread and cheese supper prepared by the Ecumenical Development Solidarity Group in the period leading up to Easter and a variety of conferences and exhibitions. A musician who is a member of the Catholic parish built an organ for the Protestant chapel; then, with a team made up of Catholics and Protestants, he built an organ for the Catholic church.

Three times a year we hold ecumenical services: on the weekend of the fair, at Christmas and on Palm Sunday (because at Easter the Cité empties and it is very difficult to gather the communities). These services reflect a slow and thoughtful evolution in which care has been taken not offend each other's convictions and traditions.

At first these services took place in the main foyer, a "neutral" space between the Protestant chapel and the Catholic church, and each stayed on its respective side. From the second year on, worship was moved to the chancel of the Catholic church, where the acoustics and visibility are better.

Instead of celebrating the eucharist and the Lord's supper one after the other, we now celebrate them simultaneously, with everyone going forward at the same time to receive communion from the priest or the pastor according to their confession. This was important for confessionally mixed couples, of whom there are an increasing number. For many years the words of institution were repeated twice. Now, only the Catholic clergy pronounce the words of institution (since it is obligatory in their tradition) and the Protestant ministers continue with the Lord's supper, using different words.

In addition, a group for mixed couples has been formed, ecumenical prayers are held every Tuesday morning and an ecumenical youth group meets every fortnight for prayer, discussion and recreational activities. While catechism in the sixth school year is not given jointly, Catholics and Protestants use the same programme. One member of the other community is present at the meetings of each parish council; and the pastors and priests meet together regularly. On Sundays, the Protestant service and the Catholic mass are held at the same time to encourage contacts before and after worship.

On the tenth anniversary of the Ecumenical Centre in 1986, the parish councils met to discuss how to give fresh impetus to ecumenism in Meyrin for the next decade. Believing that a debate on fundamental questions would help to deepen relations, we organized a day of spiritual retreat for the communities and set up an ecumenical reflection group. By this time our relations with the Evangelical Church in Meyrin had also developed, so that there are now three communities seeking a different way to live their Christian lives.

The ecumenical reflection group, after study of the World Council of Churches' Lima document on *Baptism, Eucharist and Ministry (BEM)*, concluded:

> The participants have come to believe unanimously that in the eucharist or the Lord's supper the presence of the risen Jesus Christ is real. Because of this conviction the act of communicating together is neither ambiguous nor wrong.
>
> As a practical conclusion of discussion on baptism we have started once or twice a year to hold an ecumenical baptismal service to mark our mutual recognition of baptism in a tangible way.
>
> On the basis of the important theological progress already achieved and the long spiritual journey of our Catholic, Protestant and Evangelical communities in Meyrin... the group concluded in favour of the mutual recognition of our ministries in Meyrin and the legitimacy of eucharistic hospitality.

There are several reasons that we in Meyrin have the good fortune to be able to practise our Christian faith "differently":

• The identity of each church has been respected. There is no "confessional confusion". We support one another in everything, but we respect the other's identity.

• Respect for identity is not something that "just happens". It is always necessary to listen to the other, to make a constant and conscious effort to adjust.

• This respect for mutual traditions must not mean the absence of dialogue. On the contrary, we have to challenge one another, tackle the fundamental questions and have the courage to say No. Our churches could be compared to a couple whose harmony depends on the personality of each being respected.

Two Christian congregations under the same roof. Three communities with a positive experience of living together. At the outset this was an act of faith and hope. Today it is a reality and a joy, and none of us would want to turn back the clock.

DE MERENWIJK, LEIDEN, NETHERLANDS

The Ecumenical Congregation

Geert van der Bom

When construction began in 1970 on De Merenwijk, a major new housing development in the north of the Dutch university town of Leiden, the city's council of churches called on its member churches to minister there along the lines of the so-called Lund Principle (1952): that they "act together in all matters except those in which deep differences of conviction compel them to work separately". The objective from the beginning has been to bring the churches in this new district closer together through shared communal experience, not in order to create a new "ecumenical church", but to mould a twofold solidarity — on the one hand with each person's own church, and on the other with the community experienced beyond that church in Merenwijk.

A theological advisory committee plays an important role in counselling pastors and engaging in dialogue with the participating churches. It includes theologians from the participating churches and the two local clergymen: one a Roman Catholic priest installed by the Bishop of Rotterdam, the other a Protestant minister nominated by the two large Reformed churches.

Several committees, composed of Catholics, Reformed, Lutherans and other believers, work on a day-to-day basis within the ecumenical congregation, each responsible for one aspect of the ministry. In carrying out our common responsibility, we "celebrate", "learn" and "serve". One committee is organized around each of these three key concepts, and a fourth works specifically with young people. Together with the general council of churches of Merenwijk they draw up an annual pastoral plan.

Several examples can give a hint of the life of this ecumenical community:

Hymns. There are a number of hymnals in the Netherlands. The Catholic Church alone has several different hymnbooks, while the two large Reformed churches have a common one. In our two joint Sunday services, both centring on God's word and the Lord's table, we use two hymnbooks, one Catholic and the other Reformed, which enables us to appreciate the differences and points of convergence between the two traditions. One difference, for example, can be heard in the singing of the Psalms. According to Catholic tradition, Psalms are sung in counterpoint between choir and congregation (and there are several beautiful modern versions of this). In the Reformed tradition, the whole congregation sings metrical Psalms to tunes from sixteenth-century Geneva.

Words and music can create a feeling of being "at home" in church. New residents of Merenwijk who find their way into our congregation are often enthusiastic about the inter-church co-operation at first, but are then somewhat taken aback by the challenge this entails of going beyond the limits of their own "home". Becoming involved with another kind of spiritual home — thus coming to see one's own tradition in less absolute terms — calls for an attitude of openness which many people, fortunately, are able to develop. On this basis people then also come to realize the convergence between the two traditions: for centuries now we have both been singing the songs of Israel.

A day of song, organized by the committee responsible for catechesis, sought to shed light on this background and at the same time to explain the emotional content of the hymns. While this may seem to be a relatively minor example, it highlights one of the important questions facing us: are we striving towards a "blend of traditions" according to the lowest common denominator, or are we trying to become a meeting point for the traditions? From our dealings with each other it is clear that there is hardly any real danger of a casual blending of traditions. It is more correct to say that constant contacts with members of another church lead to a deepening of the personal and the communal experience of faith.

Liturgy. What is the service of worship like? For the Reformed church members it is surprising to have a service centred not only on the word, but also on the Lord's supper every Sunday. Catholics are often surprised by the degree of reverence shown for the Scriptures. Every Sunday one of the two ministers conducts both services, always in co-operation with readers, one of the choirs and sometimes a preparatory group. The other pastor is present once on Sunday in order to say the benediction and prayer of thanksgiving. In this way the two worship services are common but different.

Anyone who enters our church can feel a homelike atmosphere. In the middle is the table, and a small pulpit stands to one side. The Easter candle is always burning and the Bible is always open. After the words of welcome, we sing a Psalm or an opening hymn, then the *Kyrie*, followed by a hymn of praise, the first and second Bible readings, which alternate with hymns, the sermon, another hymn, the offering, the Lord's supper, intercession, a closing hymn and benediction.

The influence of ecumenical dialogue in the Netherlands can be felt not only in our congregation but in many others as well. The renewed interest in the church year in the Reformed churches and the renewal of liturgy in the Catholic Church prompt us to look into a common history of over fifteen centuries. That takes us back to the common sources on which we seek to draw in our search for God who is ahead of us all.

Occasionally we encounter interesting surprises in the liturgy or elsewhere. What should we do on All Saints Day and on the preceding day which is (not by chance) Reformation day? What should we do with Protestant children who look on as their Catholic peers receive their first communion? What do we say to the asylum-seeker who wants to light a candle before the image of the Virgin Mary when from the very beginning we have never had one? In the ecumenical process, Mary became relegated to the background. There are plenty of open questions, but in our experience all of them give rise to discussion, deeper reflection and recollection. Thus, our Catholic brothers and sisters, for example, come to ask themselves what is the point of their veneration of Mary. What are saints? Others ask: can we live without examples — those persons who showed others the way in their time?

Joint house calls. The new quarter is easily divided into small blocks, and the residents are each regularly invited by the pastor to meet with one another. The committee on "Contact Persons" organizes common house calls of this kind, in which members meet with each other. Each occasion thus brings together Catholics, Reformed and even people who hardly regard themselves as believers. Everyone shares to some degree in the joys and sorrows of the community.

In this way we also regularly encounter those people who have some difficulty joining in the experience of our ecumenical congregation or who are unable to do so. Despite their own reluctance, few of them oppose this attempt at co-operation among the churches. On such evenings I always sense an unusual openness in the participants. They tell each other about the things that move and motivate them. Cares are shared, and one can sense great respect for the things that are cherished by others. Here in an ordinary housing block we experience what it can mean to walk together in faith.

We are still attached to the tradition from which we received our belief. But tradition is not a static concept, nor is it immutable. It is something active, for the handing-down of tradition is an *act*. For this reason we are always a church in the making. What has been handed down to us is a spring that quenches our thirst. Coming into contact with other, hitherto unknown sources is both a challenge and an enrichment.

We do not wish to play down the differences but to understand them with respect. We have observed that we need first of all to develop trust in each other. Only then can there be the openness that will make it possible to talk about the things that move us and are important to us. When this happens, we find that dialogue brings out the best in us, and we offer to each other the best that we have received.

9. Developing Partnership

If one member suffers, all suffer together with it; if one member is honoured, all rejoice together with it (1 Cor. 12:26).

Blessed be the God and Father of our Lord Jesus Christ, the Father of mercies and the God of all consolation, who consoles us in all our affliction, so that we may be able to console those who are in any affliction with the consolation with which we ourselves are consoled by God. For just as the sufferings of Christ are abundant for us, so also our consolation is abundant through Christ. If we are being afflicted, it is for your consolation and salvation; if we are being consoled, it is for your consolation, which you experience when you patiently endure the same sufferings that we are also suffering (2 Cor. 1:3-6).

"Now we know we are not alone. We belong to a family that goes beyond our borders. We are members of the one body of Christ. So we want to have more contacts with congregations in other countries."

This affirmation — from the Potsdam Ecumenical Gathering of Congregational Groups in July 1993 — of belonging to a worldwide family needs to be confirmed through practical experience again and again. Ecumenical partnership relations with a congregation in another country and perhaps of another confession are the best way to experience that we are in fact not alone. Exchange of experiences and concerns, mutual encouragement and inspiration, as well as direct mutual help, contribute to a common growth in faith and in love.

- How is your local congregation experiencing its relation to the worldwide Christian family?
- What are the subjects of exchange in the existing partnership relations of your congregation?
- How does your congregation prevent its partnerships from becoming one-sided donor-receiver relations?

BLOMBERG, GERMANY

A German-South African Partnership

Ulrich Möller

Over a period of some seven years, a covenanting partnership with a South African congregation in the township of Duduza, southeast of Johannesburg, became a very special opportunity for ecumenical learning and sharing for the Reformed congregation in Blomberg, Germany, and an occasion for congregational renewal.

Blomberg is a small town in the district of Lippe in the state of North Rhine-Westphalia. The town and the surrounding villages have a population of about 10,000. Two relatively large enterprises in Blomberg and a smaller neighbouring town are of particular economic importance for the region, each providing some 2500 jobs. A Dutch NATO anti-aircraft unit was stationed in Blomberg, and about 3000 Dutch lived in the town, but since 1990 this unit has been gradually disbanded. Beginning in the mid-1980s there has been an influx of migrant families, particularly from the former Soviet Union, and up to 250 refugees, especially Kurds, Indians and Pakistanis, live in municipal hostels for asylum-seekers.

The Reformed congregation in Blomberg has something like 4800 members, and the social stratification of the population of Blomberg is also reflected in its composition. There has been no strong tradition of religious observance in the past. In many families church traditions have virtually ceased to exist. Church membership is taken for granted by most members of the congregation but very few express it by regular church attendance. The members involved in the life of the congregation are predominantly middle class.

The congregation runs a nursery and helps to support an ecumenical centre for diakonia together with the neighbouring congregations. A woman staff member works full-time with children and young people. Ecumenical cooperation, especially with the Dutch congregations, has included services for the World Day of Prayer and Ascension Day, Ecumenical Bible Week, meditations for Holy Week, joint sponsorship of a centre for the unemployed and a centre for diakonia, church music, the ministerial association and ecumenical youth movements in the context of a German-Dutch town-twinning arrangement. For many years there has been a partnership with the Reformed congregation in the town of Brandenburg in the former German Democratic Republic.

Steps towards renewal

As early as the mid-1970s the parish council urged the congregation to open up to social challenges. But it proved difficult to communicate to the wider congregation the commitment represented, for instance, by a meeting of a peace group or Amnesty International chapter in the parish hall. Basically, each congregational group concentrated on its own identity, and awareness of an identity as a whole congregation was not very well developed.

A crisis in the congregation in the 1980s, occasioned by a change of minister and personal conflicts, led the elders and the new minister to seek a new approach to congregational renewal. There was a very practical determination to get over the disillusionment and frustration and revive a sense of fellowship by encouraging the disillusioned and non-involved to come and join in the work of a congregation with which they could identify.

The church council saw the crisis also as a spiritual challenge. It asked what promise and commission the congregation had received and what the resulting prospects were in the existing situation. What follows from the fact that Jesus Christ is the foundation that upholds our congregation (1 Cor. 3:11)? God's Spirit enables us to work together as members of the one body of Christ for the upbuilding of the congregation (1 Cor. 12:11-27). If we want to relate this promise realistically to our congregation, what practical forms can we discover to enable everyone — men and women, old and young — to work together on an equal footing?

With the help of the pastors, the parish council examined different models for promoting congregational life. It officially adopted a theological framework and fundamental goals to give the congregation a focus for its self-understanding. These were published in the parish newsletter, as were all the further steps towards congregational renewal. From the beginning a trainer from outside supported the parish council, helping to establish common priorities in such a way that everyone could contribute his or her own point of view without feeling dominated by the pastors. Four fundamental objectives for further congregational work received special priority. First (by a long way) came the goal: "Our congregation supports justice, peace and the integrity of creation"; then came: "The Word of God has meaning for our everyday lives", "The congregation is there for the weak" and "Worship is central".

Workers from all areas of the congregation's activities were then invited to a weekend meeting to reflect on what it would mean in practice to focus on these goals in the different facets of congregational life. Participants in this meeting experienced a deep sense of spiritual fellowship which inspired them to carry the visions they shared for the life of the congregation into daily life and to create structures to realize them in the form of regular congregational gatherings. Meetings and social events for church workers were arranged to strengthen exchange and fellowship, and it was decided to hold a meeting for the promotion of congregational life at least every two years.

It was important for us always to look critically at what we were doing and ask ourselves questions like these: How can we guard against expecting too much of ourselves and others in our efforts for renewal? How can we leave room for the working of the Holy Spirit and not lapse into false activism? How can we take seriously the knowledge that it is not we but God himself who upbuilds and sustains his people, and that only in this way will God's blessing rest on what we do?

In all the different congregational activities great enthusiasm then went into trying to reshape what already existed to embody the goals defined. This was reflected, for example, in a celebration of the Lord's supper focused on fellowship, in a greater emphasis on music in children's services and in more cooperation in the musical field with the other local congregations. Many initiatives were taken to strengthen fellowship among the children and young people of the congregation. A special project to involve parents in church education led to a new form of confirmation class. A group of visitors for old and sick members of the congregation was formed, and various other projects were organized to create greater contact between young and old members of the congregation. The congregation's work in diakonia opened up to the troubles of asylum-seekers and migrants in Blomberg, first on a voluntary basis, then with a full-time involvement.

Many encouraging things happened. Many members found a way back into "their" congregation, even people who saw themselves as rather on the edge of things. Of course there were also dead-ends and setbacks. But above all the life of the congregation not only became richer, more lively and diversified but also more complex and difficult. Where originally we were complaining about the lack of workers, we soon had so many committed people working together in the congregation that the pastors faced the new challenge of providing spiritual support for the many workers and being involved with the different groups. The increased activity also made it necessary to build a substantial extension to the parish hall.

To deal with the variety of new demands, it was decided that the work of the leadership should be supported by continual professional advice. Without such a chance for the pastors and the president of the parish council to review the now very complex work monthly with an outside expert, promoting congregational life might very well have bogged down. For all of us constantly carry our human weaknesses around with us and wound each other even when we are trying to promote the life of God's people. Handling these disputes frankly and in a spirit of fellowship called for a difficult and at times also painful learning process.

In the years that followed there were many reasons to thank God for his sustaining presence in these new beginnings. But our experience was not unlike that of the people of Israel after the exodus. When the waterless tracts of the journey appear, we soon forget how our new departure has liberated us from what had been holding us prisoner and paralyzing us. Frank discussion, grumbling and argument about these waterless tracts was important. And so we had another meeting for promoting congregational life under the theme of "crossing the wilderness". Using passages from the book of Exodus, we tried to understand our own journey, with its new departures and its waterless stretches, as a path trodden under God and with God.

People were able to express criticism and frustration over friction points in the relations among the greatly increased number of workers. We recognized that moving from mere "grumbling" to "complaining before the Lord" was the only way for us to overcome difficult times in fellowship with God. Even more important than the many practical proposals for improving cooperation in the congregation were our attempts to find wellsprings of spiritual strength in our community. Besides new approaches to worship it was felt to be important to find space for a fellowship room in the extended parish hall, where individuals and groups could take time out to come together spontaneously and creatively and gain new strength and new outlooks in talking with God, meditation and worship.

A covenanting partnership with Duduza

A special opportunity for ecumenical congregational renewal presented itself to the congregation as a result of the partnership begun in 1987 with the Reformed congregation of the black South African township of Duduza. In 1986 the *Belydende Kring*, the confessing movement of the South African Reformed churches, had suggested such covenants between congregations to the member churches of the World Alliance of Reformed Churches, seeing this as a way to strengthen those congregations that were taking a confessing stance against apartheid and seeking to free themselves from dependence on the whites. Our parish council saw a partnership of this kind as an opportunity to implement in practice our commitment to the conciliar process for justice, peace and the integrity of creation. We entered the partnership along with the congregation of the neighbouring village of Wöbbel. The surrounding congregations in the district also support and encourage the partnership.

In 1983 a massacre by government security forces had taken place in Duduza in response to peaceful protests, and a state of emergency was declared. In the years of severe oppression that followed, the Reformed congregation, led by its pastor Hendrik Maphanga, had developed into a committed advocate of the oppressed and had started various projects for the victims of apartheid. Taking advantage of the financial dependence of the black congregation (in an area of more than 60 percent unemployment), the white "mother church" thereupon tried to divert the congregation in Duduza from its confessing stance by financial blackmail. Here the partnership intervened: the two German congregations undertook for a period of up to ten years to provide the Duduza congregation with the finance which had till then been given by the white church. The intent was to make the congregation impervious to blackmail in its effort to witness for truth and justice. To ensure that the partnership could develop without being dominated by financial considerations, the money was not sent directly but paid into a fund of the *Belydende Kring*. The ten-year limit on financial support was meant to prevent a new dependence from developing.

We in Blomberg and Wöbbel hoped for new opportunities of ecumenical learning from this partnership. As a congregation of a national church in a First World country, we wanted to learn from the witness of a confessing congregation in the Third World, to understand each other as members of the one body of Christ, to get beyond our own provincialism and take on our share of responsibility for Christian witness in the one world, in personal interchange with our brothers and sisters in Duduza. From the start our partner congregation likewise affirmed that spiritual fellowship was the common foundation for our mutually helping each other to bear the witness enjoined upon us in our respective situations — even beyond the day of liberation in South Africa.

Soon after our initial contacts with Duduza, the partnership was sealed officially with the general secretary of the *Belydende Kring* at a congregational event, in a celebration of the Lord's supper. A joint "Duduza Partnership Group" was founded in order to establish the partnership firmly through information about the political and church situation in South Africa; contacts with Duduza by way of letters, photographs, audio- and video-cassettes; personal encounters; and publicity in the local and church press and through informative events, services of intercession and special campaigns of solidarity.

In the first few years it was very difficult to make direct contact with the people in Duduza. Sometimes letters were intercepted by the South African authorities, and our partners in Duduza found letters an even more a difficult means of communication than we did. This led to some disappointments and a barren period. Because we were anxious to avoid "church tourism" we decided not to make direct congregational visits until intensive partnership work had been done in other fields. We managed to maintain this principle by taking advantage of opportunities provided by the networks surrounding our partnership on both sides. We invited several South African church delegations visiting Germany to come to our congregations, and they in turn were able to establish links with and to Duduza through the *Belydende Kring*. In 1990 Pastor Maphanga's first visit to Lippe was a real breakthrough. When at the end of his visit he summarized his impressions by saying, "My days with you have shown me that Christ has brought us together into a real fellowship", many of our members felt the same. In the years that followed, we could now put a living face and voice to our partner congregation.

During the 1980s the Reformed congregation in Duduza had found itself in a pioneering role in the struggle against apartheid, which constantly exceeded the capacity of the premises at its disposal. Not only all the congregational events, but also free legal consultations and practically all the major political gatherings of independent organizations in the township of some 50,000 took place in its church. The congregation was therefore pressing for the building of a community centre.

The stage of partnership work that followed focused on planning in Duduza and canvassing for support for the project in Lippe. The partnership group put together an exhibition about Duduza. The Blomberg schools held a competition to design a poster, and at the German Protestant Kirchentag in Essen in 1991 the campaign "A Stone for

Duduza" was inaugurated. People were asked to link their financial support with personal expressions of solidarity painted on clay bricks.

To show the congregation in Duduza that personal encounter and solidarity were more important to us than money in supporting the project, the partnership group decided to go to Duduza with a group of young adults in May 1993 for a work camp of several weeks. Those taking part experienced how fragile hope is for people whose visions of a better life are constantly stifled by South Africa's everyday violence. The very fact that the group came to Duduza made hope flicker afresh for many. As they worked together on the building site, talked together and attended worship, new seeds of hope grew visibly. The young people came back to Blomberg different from when they set off. For the people in Duduza the partnership is now one of many faces, and new friendships have developed.

Given the gap in wealth, how can we continue to journey together as equal members of the one body of Christ and help each other to bear witness? The joint project and the mutual commitment that goes along with it offer many opportunities for learning in this respect. But many snares also remain. We shall manage to avoid them only if the congregations can increasingly share their strengths and weaknesses with one another — if we manage to show our own weakness without at once calling forth the other's strength — and if we manage really to establish the work on a broad base in the congregations through partnership groups on both sides. But this also means that the challenge from the respective partners must make us take a sharper look at our own congregation and its local situation. So it was only logical that the Blomberg congregation has not only been concerned with racism in South Africa but has also taken a stand against xenophobia and hostility to foreigners locally. Work in solidarity with asylum-seekers and support for migrants from former East-bloc countries in their difficult process of integration are part of this.

The experiences so far in reaching out across boundaries have encouraged the partner congregations and also a number of others to believe that there is promise for the future in the song of prayer for partnership: "Bind us together, Lord, bind us together with cords that cannot be broken. Bind us together, Lord, bind us together with love. There is only one God. There is only one King. There is only one Body. That is why we can sing: Bind us together, Lord…"

GUBEN (GERMANY) AND GUBIN (POLAND)

Neighbours Must Become Neighbours

Wolfram Schulz

The River Neisse, which has formed the border between Germany and Poland since 1945, snakes its way through meadows and forests. Behind its two banks rise the roofs of villages that still bear the marks of the war that raged to an end here some 50 years ago.

Access roads to former bridges now lead nowhere. The only bridges for miles around are the highway bridge near Forst and the Stadtbrücke linking Guben and Gubin, some 15 kilometres before the junction of the Neisse and the Oder. Traffic reports warn of 20, 30 or even 50 hours' waiting time for lorries. It goes somewhat more quickly for cars, and pedestrians and cyclists need only a few minutes — and then, in less than 100 metres, you are in the other town, whose name is almost identical, the two having once been one and the same town.

Before 1945 this town proudly called itself "the Pearl of the Niederlausitz". Blossoming fruit-trees on the hills lured countless visitors in the spring; the cloth and the hats from its factories were exported to many countries; the theatre on the Neisse island bore witness to city's self-confidence. In the now-Polish Old Town, war has left behind only the dramatic ruins of the Hauptkirche and the remains of the town hall. On the German side, there is a small segment of the Old Town and areas of new buildings dating back to the 1950s. The hat and cloth industry took the form of state co-operatives until the fall of the Wall put an end to that; since 1961 there has been a synthetic fibre factory here but the number of workers has dwindled to 10 percent of its full capacity.

The border with Poland has again been open to us only since 1989 after being closed by the German Democratic Republic authorities at the beginning of the 1980s. For our Polish neighbours, the problems lasted even longer. So when we Gubeners and Gubiners do cross the bridge, what are we looking for? Most people go to shop, over there at a market, over here in a supermarket. Just going for a walk, visiting friends, taking in a concert or a discotheque are all still the exceptions, important though they may be.

The fact is that the neighbours hardly know each other — and how could they? Only very few are familiar with the others' language, as there is no tradition of neighbourly relations here. The older folk who have lived here since before 1945 remember when the whole area was entirely inside Germany and Poland was far away. The older citizens on the other side of the Neisse were resettled there after 1945, mostly from eastern Poland. Their native region was far from Germany, and if they have any knowledge of German, it is associated with memories of the German assault on and occupation of Poland, forced labour or worse.

In any case, there are only very few of those older folk still around, and the young people have had no opportunities for contact up to now. Yet, until most businesses closed down, about a thousand Poles worked on the German side. Some had lodgings here; others crossed the bridge every day, either on foot or by bus. A few ties of friendship still survive here and there. Who, then, crosses the bridge for reasons other than shopping? Some Poles have found work here in construction companies, so they come across; then there are other persons who are either victims or beneficiaries of the incredible gap in prosperity between the two sides of the border. Some people rummage through garbage for items of furniture or clothing — a shame on both nations, though even more shameful are the remarks heard about this from some Germans. And then there are others who harbour designs on bicycles, cars, weekend homes or insufficiently secured doors. On account of them, old prejudices are flourishing once again.

This makes any positive neighbourly experience all the more significant and worth recounting: for example, when people have visited their former homes and have received and accepted a friendly welcome in the houses they once occupied. In such cases, people have come together in friendship — and where language fails, signs take over — after a history that makes friendship look like a miracle. When an eighty-year-old former occupant, speaking through a neighbour as interpreter, calms the fears of the present farmer saying, "Zofia, that house belongs to you now and it should stay that way", then there is hope. Should it not be possible for good neighbourly relations to thrive between the people of Gubin and Guben?

This was the question Christians asked themselves on Boxing Day 1989, when they assembled by candlelight on either side of the bridge. That encounter has since become an annual tradition. Christians of all confessions invite each other to attend. Admittedly, we no longer have more than 1000 people, as in the beginning, but for some time now this is no longer the only occasion for contact between the two towns.

Each year, on an alternating basis, the event begins with a bilingual worship service, either at the St Trinitatis Catholic Church in Gubin or at the Protestant Klosterkirche in Guben. A candlelight procession then sets out for the meeting place on the Neisse bridge, which is closed to traffic for half an hour. Since bad weather is not unusual at this time of year, some candles are constantly blown out, giving rise to a beautiful and memorable experience: someone is always nearby with a candle still burning. The act of lighting and relighting each other's candles has become the real liturgy of the encounter. We believe this is how it really ought to be; we should constantly give light to each other again, as no one can keep it for himself or herself alone. Addresses are sometimes exchanged and visits agreed on.

Pupils from Gubin attend the high school in Guben. The Lutheran hospital in Guben has a partnership with the Gubin hospital. Together, pupils from both towns have started clean-up work on the Neisse island, where a centre for Polish-German encounter is to be built on the site of the destroyed city theatre. Young people tinker about together at a motor bike club. From time to time, the Klosterkirche choir sings at the Catholic church in Gubin, and the Corpus Christi procession sets out from there for the Guben church square. Polish children are invited to the feast of St Martin, which is an ecumenical celebration.

The older members of our congregation were once invited to a children's fair, at which the priest introduced us to the children: "These are Protestant Christians who were once baptized here in the big Stadt-kirche." We said to the children: "You will rebuild the church from the ruins on the marketplace. We hope that you will be able to do so, and you should take it as your church — together with the statue of Guben mayor J.W. Franck, who composed the hymn 'Jesus, priceless treasure' here."

As both towns now officially aspire to become a European twin city, Christians also see this as a matter of concern to them, for which they can do a lot together. In May 1993, there was a small European encounter of partner congregations from the Protestant communities in the Czech Republic, Poland, the Rhineland and the Netherlands. On that occasion, we bore testimony to the hope that the European house would be filled by the Spirit, which we have known from ties of friendship over many decades as the Spirit of sharing with each other, and which, we are confident, will also make the neighbours on the Neisse into true neigh-bours.

10. Not a Dream Church, but Churches with Dreams

Antonio Carlos de Melo Magelhaes

Sometimes when I worship in German congregations I have the feeling that real life and people have been left outside the door. A liturgy which has lost its appeal and become detached from everyday reality is followed Sunday after Sunday without having any real connection with people's lives. The presumed reasons for society's estrangement from or general indifference to the church are often repeated: the process of secularization, the consequences of the intellectual tradition of the Enlightenment. I believe these are issues that have to be tackled seriously, but I do not consider these to be a sufficient excuse for the church's inaction and its lack of options or alternatives.

It is too easy to blame the church's loss of significance on purely external factors. The fact that there is a long-standing process of secularization in Europe whose effects will continue to be felt in the future does not in itself explain why the church no longer has anything to say to people in relation to their problems, anxieties and dreams. It is not the only reason why the "folk church" has become a church without folk. In fact the secularization process has not meant the end of religion in Europe but rather society's estrangement from the church. Religion and religious feeling are flourishing in Europe. They are expressed in new religious movements unconnected with the Christian tradition, in Christian groups outside the established church and even in consumer-oriented bodies that offer a religion based on feelings without ethics, prayer without just action and worship without empathy and sympathy for one's neighbours.

Many of the case studies in the book make it clear that a lively and committed congregation cannot develop where the priority is given to established structures. A lively and renewed community will begin to emerge only when the people start to reflect on their spiritual and intellectual situation in the widest sense and alter it in the light of their faith. The church can exist as a healing community concerned for

Antonio Carlos de Melo Magelhaes teaches at the Ecumenical Institute for Postgraduate Studies of Theology and Science of Religion in São Paulo, Brazil. Earlier he taught at the Mission Academy in Hamburg, Germany.

spirituality and human needs only if it takes its own context and environment seriously and works creatively and imaginatively in the local situation, like the Bromley-by-Bow Neighbourhood Church. Whatever the work, be it with children or with artists, it is impossible to follow a single model; the appropriate model has to be thought out and adapted to each situation and context. But the first step is always the same: a congregation allows itself to be "provoked" by the situation of the people in its own context, creates space and an inviting atmosphere and in turn provokes those around it by its proclamation of the good news.

Crossing boundaries in church action

In practice there are two models for crossing boundaries in church action. The first moves from the usual group attending worship to other (fringe) groups. These may be children, as in the Lutheran congregation in Budapest, or refugees, as in Vallentuna. Such groups bring their own questions, problems and ideas into the life of the congregation.

If a congregation revolves exclusively around its familiar circle of members, it will in time become increasingly closed to new ideas and ways of doing things. Openness towards other groups is more than a sociological process involving renewal of an established community; it is a mission laid on the church by the gospel, which it may not neglect. Crossing borders in this sense implies two ecclesiological-theological aspects:

1. It is linked to the evangelizing task of the church, which consists in making manifest the symbols of the church and proclaiming the gospel in its most fundamental sense as good news while at the same time challenging people to a change of mind, to conversion. A church which cannot responsibly carry out this task with joy and conviction is a long way from its missionary duty.

2. Before turning towards other groups in this way there must be a decision at the ecclesiological-theological level always to give the marginalized groups priority. This option is taken for the sake of the gospel itself, which is above all good news to the suffering and excluded.

There are two dangers in this cross-border outreach. On the one hand, the task of evangelism may be confused with proselytism or church expansionism; on the other, a church which is still dominated by the middle classes may no longer able to proclaim the wholeness of the gospel and to liberate itself from subjective bourgeois religion based on inner satisfaction.

Of course, this kind of outreach seldom takes place without conflict and friction in the congregation. Work with new groups cannot always be done harmoniously. Willingness to accept such widening of horizons must already exist in the congregation or else it must be created in the process of opening up to these groups. One thing is certain: there can be no ecumenical renewal of a congregation if people do not find the courage to take these steps.

The second model for crossing borders is partnership and cooperation with congregations from other contexts. An example of this is the congregation in Blomberg/Lippe, and its effects on the work there have been admirably described. Let me emphasize two points in relation to this example:

1. Partnership cannot be an escape mechanism for congregations in the affluent world which have grown rich partly because of unfair trading and injustice in the world. Fraternal relations between congregations here and in impoverished regions must be seen and felt to be a sign of the great commission laid on all in the body of Christ. They should not be reduced to the schema of culprit (here)/victim (there), or subject (here)/object (there).

2. Partnership between a congregation in Europe and a congregation in another context should be an opportunity to discover the situation of foreigners in one's own country, not a substitute for taking on tasks close to home. Only a congregation which is open and willing to cross borders in this way can pray "Only one Lord. Only one God. Only one Body. That is why can sing, bind us together, Lord..."

A living congregation is not a safe haven

It is clear from these reports that congregational renewal should not be confused with enthusiastic participation in church rites and evangelization campaigns. Christian faith does of course include enthusiasm and inner "fire", but it cannot be reduced to that alone. The power of the Holy Spirit shows itself above all in friendly congregations who are in close touch with the world around them and understand their proclamation and practice as good news.

Congregational renewal contains a spirituality which can accept neither a "bureaucratic" church nor privatized religion. This spirituality is directed towards fellowship and community; it is not private and individual and not exclusively concerned with the "soul". It thus expresses the experience of God in the place where the congregation lives, and because it rests on the experience of God it is personal. Furthermore, this is an incarnate, concrete, visible spirituality which is open to the situations, conflicts and dreams of real people. Even if this spirituality has taken flesh, it is still of the Spirit. In short, without real, practical life there can be no spiritual life either.

When Christian communities and congregations begin to allow themselves to be renewed by the Holy Spirit and by the context in which they live, the credibility of the Christian community is strengthened. Without renewed congregations there can be no practical and realistic theology and no good news of the gospel. When we dream of a new church and a new theology, we depend on local congregations and churches.

No such thing as a dream church exists. What does exist are local churches and congregations which in the power of the Holy Spirit have the courage to dream of a new church. Their experience and practice are crucial if we want to speak of renewal.

11. Congregational Renewal in Europe: An African Perspective

John D.K. Ekem

As an ordained minister of the Methodist Church of Ghana, West Africa, it is impossible for me to speak authentically for the whole of Africa, given the complex social, religious, political and economic pluralism which characterizes that suffering continent. Rather, I shall locate my remarks in the context of Europe's encounter with sub-Saharan Africa since the fifteenth century and the far-reaching consequences of that for the peoples of this sub-region. Five years in Germany have deepened my impressions of this encounter and its tremendous challenges for churches in Europe. I do not intend to engage in a polemic against Europe and its churches but to help promote a new sense of responsibility among European Christians about their prophetic role in correcting various forms of structural injustice in other parts of our globe.

Hearing what the Spirit says

Hearing what the Spirit says to us in this present age involves coming out of our protective shells of comfortable, self-enriching routines to allow God's Spirit to guide us to explore new avenues of responsible service for the needy outside our gates. The one who has promised to make all things new (Rev. 21:5) invites us to be his co-workers in fulfilling this eschatological hope as expressed in the Lord's prayer: "Your kingdom come. Your will be done, on earth as it is in heaven" (Matt. 6:10). This implies what we refer to in Wesleyan Methodist circles as the cultivation of *social holiness*: the experience of divine forgiveness and renewal which inspires us to face up squarely to specific challenges confronting us in our contemporary situations, not in silent and passive contemplation, but in positive action towards the accomplishment of God's salutary purposes for his creation.

Europe's Christian congregations are currently faced with the delicate task of seeking renewal in obedient and discerning response to the voice

John Ekem is a pastor of the Methodist Church in Ghana and teaches at the University of Accra. Earlier he was on the staff of the Mission Academy in Hamburg.

of God's Spirit in an age of increasing secularism, social and political upheaval and economic recession on their continent. Addressing these domestic challenges together with those coming from other parts of the globe requires an endowment with special divine resources, a humble appropriation of God's promise to Zerubbabel through the prophet Zechariah: "Not by might, nor by power, but by my Spirit, says the Lord of hosts" (Zech. 4:6). Churches in Europe are thereby being called upon critically to re-examine aspects of the post-Enlightenment heritage that tend to marginalize divine involvement in human affairs. Here much could probably be learned from traditional African spirituality, in which the empirical and meta-empirical worlds are closely linked with each other and human actions based on common-sense experience are understood as deriving their ultimate validity from an encounter with the *mysterium tremendum et fascinosum*.

Viewing Christian Europe with African spectacles

No honest African church historian can deny the active role of European Christian missions in the planting and growth of Christianity, especially within sub-Saharan Africa. We salute those missionaries who risked their lives in proclaiming the gospel to our people, learning the indigenous languages and reducing them to writing, setting up schools, hospitals and other infrastructural networks that have become important legacies for many independent African states.

But there is another side to the coin: the Christianization of sub-Saharan Africa went hand in hand with its colonization and exploitation by European powers who usually found allies in Christian missionaries from their home countries. Many were imbued with a sense of cultural superiority and a Eurocentrism that had no respect for cultural values other than their own. Accepting their version of Christianity meant in effect abandoning one's own roots to adopt an "artificial" European identity. This "identity-crisis" has haunted European mission-founded churches up to the present day, and the emergence of African Independent Churches is partly traceable to it. Nevertheless, those of us who have inherited the legacies left by European Christian missions are greatly troubled by the alarming rate at which Europe is being de-Christianized in the wake of secularization and dissociation from creeds, dogmas and ecclesiastical structures that have long since lost their relevance for large sections of the population.

It has in fact been contended in certain circles that the time has come for Europe to be evangelized by African Christian missionaries in whose regions Christianity has become the dominant religion. Congregational renewal in Europe should entail among other things the humility to admit these deficits and the willingness to learn from others whose worldviews have hitherto not been taken seriously, on the principles of mutual respect and reciprocal challenge.

One must also not overlook the role of European Christian missions in the economic exploitation and socio-political destabilization of several African communities. For example, chaplains of Portuguese, Dutch and English trade stations that operated in the Gold Coast (Ghana) between the fifteenth and eighteenth centuries were intensely pre-occupied with the horrifying slave trade, which sapped Africa of its valuable human resources and precipitated social and political unrest while helping to create huge amounts of capital for Europe's development. If the nineteenth-century missionary drive in sub-Saharan Africa was governed in part by the desire to "compensate" the region by introducing the benefits of European civilization — such as road and rail networks — these were also used by European colonial agents to exploit the indigenous peoples' natural resources in order to generate capital for the colonial powers. This ongoing exploitative system has contributed immensely to the current economic prosperity of Western Europe and its allies. Many churches in Europe are entangled in this tragic situation, for their incomes and investments are linked to questionable gains accruing from the contemporary world economic order. Congregational renewal in a European context should seriously address this issue, which is having devastating effects on many so-called Third World countries and damaging the vestiges of Europe's Christian identity in the eyes of our suffering peoples.

We appeal to our Christian brothers and sisters in Europe to re-examine their commitment to the gospel message of love towards one's neighbour, including those who do not necessarily belong to our circle of acquaintance (cf. Luke 10:25-37), which leads to respect for and practice of the Golden Rule. This is a call to the practice of what could be labelled the ecumenics of restitution: a conscious effort, by the enabling power of God's Spirit, to help restore that which has been taken away from the damaged party. Only then can genuine koinonia take place.

What practical implications do these remarks have for European congregations? It is obvious that Europe's congregations cannot ignore the burning questions of environmental destruction in poor countries resulting from the reckless exploitation of their natural resources, refugees escaping economic doom and political oppression, debt crises strangling nations compelled by human systems to be on the borrowing end, huge sums of poor nations' hard-earned money locked up in European banks by selfish stooges of the neo-colonialists who have no interest at all in the welfare of their suffering peoples. Listening to what the Spirit says means mustering the courage to challenge governments and policy-makers to *metanoia* from the legitimization of unjust social, economic and political structures created in the interest of a section of humanity. It is a call to the realization that the earth and all that is in it have been entrusted to us *all* for proper stewardship and that we are keepers of one another.

Congregational renewal in Europe should be profoundly prophetic, given such challenges facing Europe's churches. Churches in Africa and elsewhere are of course not free from error or exempt from responsibility. Each of us is vulnerable to sins of *omission* as well as *commission*. As members of the church militant, let us cultivate the spirit of mutual learning and exhort, admonish and correct one another in love. May the peace of God be with us all, and may our ears be opened to hear what God's Spirit is saying to us in these critical times.

12. Listening to the Spirit

Kosuke Koyama

In the beginning, "a wind (spirit) from God swept over the face of the waters" (Gen. 1:2). This is the beginning of the universal church in which the *cosmos* (universe) is *ecclesia* (church), and *ecclesia* is *cosmos*. "The whole earth is full of God's glory" (Isa. 6:3). Jesus, who said "foxes have holes, and birds of the air have nests, but the Son of Man has nowhere to lay his head" (Luke 9:58), is the "fullness of God's glory" (John 1:14; cf. Heb. 1:3). This is a great evangelical puzzle. The homeless Christ (John 1:11) is the home for both *cosmos* and *ecclesia*. What does this paradox reveal about the nature of the Christian congregation?

The homelessness of Christ demonstrates the intensity of the self-giving love of God. For the sake of others, he gives up his "home". There is no deception or illusion about this. He does not give grudgingly nor does he suffer from a persecution complex. How is Christ's congregation to follow this Christ? What kind of dedication is Jesus calling for when he says that "no one who puts a hand to the plough and looks back is fit for the kingdom of God" (Luke 9:62)? When the congregation follows the knocked about, crucified Christ, it also will be knocked about. It belongs to the essence of love to be "knocked about". Love is ever active. It cannot settle down.

Christ's congregations are scattered throughout the world. They speak in thousands of different languages. According to the *World Christian Encyclopaedia* there are 8990 distinct people groups. This means that there could be 8990 distinctive theological cultures in the world! The body of Christ, the church, comprises an amazing variety of human conditions.

To each congregation the Spirit of God speaks words that are both universal and contextual. We fail to discern the gravity of these words if we do not understand the tragic reality of the global human condition. Roughly 3500 million of the 5500 million people on this planet are

Kosuke Koyama from Japan is professor of Ecumenics and World Christianity at Union Theological Seminary in New York. This essay is based on his keynote address at the Potsdam consultation.

subjected to the chronic and debilitating misery of poverty. Most of them spend all their time and energy just managing to survive. For the comfort of 2000 million people, the rest of humanity and vast natural resources are ruthlessly exploited, knocked about and knocked out. Earth's biosphere is irretrievably polluted. The world is hopelessly messy and tragic. It is replete with the cries of bitterness and resentment of the oppressed, both living and dead (Gen. 4:10). Yet the Holy Spirit has not abandoned the world. The congregation is created anew every morning (Lam. 3:22f.).

It is against this global background that the worshipping congregation hears the words of the Spirit. In congregational Bible study it hears the voice of the Spirit. When a congregational committee meeting opens with the prayer, "Come, Holy Spirit, fill all life with your radiance!", the committee on behalf of the congregation listens to what the Spirit has to say. "Let anyone who has an ear listen to what the Spirit is saying to the churches" (Rev. 2, 3).

What is it the Spirit is saying to us? What are the criteria by which we know that we are listening to the Spirit of God and not to some unclean spirits? To respond to this question, I shall be guided by the image of the congregation whose head is the Christ who has nowhere to lay his head. Our criteria are hidden in the homeless Christ.

Christ's congregation trusts in God and practises love in the name of God, however imperfectly. It must not trust in the devil or practise hate. Without the prayerful intention of trusting in God and practising love, there is no point in asking about such criteria. Trusting in God and practising love may invite the possibility of martyrdom. Ultimately, then, all Christian criteria point to martyrdom. "You will be my witnesses" — *martyres* (Acts 1:8). "When the days drew near for him to be taken up, he set his face to go to Jerusalem" (Luke 9:51). From the face of Jesus, set to go to Jerusalem to suffer, come the ultimate criteria for the discernment of the true Spirit.

The Spirit is free. The Spirit is sovereign. We do not and cannot decide what the Spirit would say to the church. Yet the Spirit speaks to the church through the Scripture and Tradition in the continuous life of a Christian congregation. "We trust in God the Holy Spirit," declares the Brief Statement of Faith by the Presbyterian Church USA (1990):

We trust in God the Holy Spirit,
   everywhere the giver and renewer of life.

The Spirit justifies us by grace through faith,
   sets us free to accept ourselves and to love God and neighbour,

and binds us together with all believers
in the one body of Christ, the church.

The same Spirit
who inspired the prophets and apostles
rules our faith and life in Christ through Scripture,
engages us through the word proclaimed,
claims us in the waters of baptism,
feeds us with the bread of life and the cup of salvation,
and calls women and men to all ministries of the church.

In a broken and fearful world
the Spirit gives us courage
to pray without ceasing,
to witness among all peoples to Christ as Lord and Saviour,
to unmask idolatries in church and culture,
to hear the voices of peoples long silenced,
and to work with others for justice, freedom and peace.

In gratitude to God, empowered by the Spirit,
we strive to serve Christ in our daily tasks
and to live holy and joyful lives,
even as we watch for God's new heaven and new earth,
praying, "Come, Lord Jesus!"

In this way Presbyterians have expressed their faith in God the Holy Spirit who comes to us, abides with us, sustains us, helps us, instructs us, purifies us and empowers us. The Spirit speaks to us.

In deep humility we say that it is beyond our ability to grasp all the wonderful ways in which the Spirit is speaking to us. But let me try to outline three fragments of what I think the Spirit may be saying to the churches in this time.

1. The Spirit seems to be saying to us: break the boundaries

Jesus eliminates the boundaries set up by human greed and self-righteousness. Anyone who prays, "God, I thank you that I am not like other people" (Luke 18:11), sets up boundaries. Jesus is against boundaries that increase oppression, war, slavery, casteism, genocide, exclusion and exploitation. Speaking to a Samaritan woman he breaks the boundary of an accepted social convention; healing a sick man on the sabbath, he breaks the boundary of religious observance; accepting an invitation from the chief tax collector, he breaks the boundary of political animosity; being crucified, he tears the boundary curtain of the temple in two. And appearing to the disciples after his death on the cross he breaks the ultimate boundary of life and death. Jesus Christ publicly breaks the boundaries set up by human greed and self-righteousness. Christian faith is based on a public, not a secret story.

Nearly all boundaries are erected by those who want to subjugate others in order to demonstrate their own superiority. Racism creates a boundary that ensures the superiority of dominant racial groups. Land-grabbing Americans in the nineteenth century called the native people "devils in human shape". Racial boundaries are a work of the unclean spirit (Mark 9:14-29). Boundaries between men and women drawn by the unclean spirit perpetuate the subjugation of women. A similar boundary was erected between the cultures of East and West to express the superiority of Western culture.

Even between religions, boundaries erected piously are used to exalt one's own religion over others. Proselytism represents a boundary of self-righteousness between one's own position and that of others. Prosely-tizers denigrate other religions in order to propagate their own faith. Militarism survives by drawing and redrawing the boundary between friend and enemy. The boundary between the poor and the rich makes the unclean spirit of exploitation happy.

All these "isms" pollute human community. They are works of the unclean spirit. Jesus cast them out, and his congregation must battle against them also.

2. The Spirit seems to be saying to us: be of the same mind

Within the Christian congregation itself confusing boundaries are drawn over many issues that impinge on our life today. Some Christians consider homosexuality to be a sinful life-style, while others feel that it is legitimate. Some Christians are saying that women should be ordained to the ministry, while others disagree. Some call for the use of inclusive language in the liturgy, while others reject it. Some accept abortion, while others condemn it. Some agree with euthanasia, while others are repelled by it. Some favour higher taxes on the affluent, while others object to any tax increase. Some call for lenient immigration laws, while others demand stricter laws. Some approve huge military expenditures, while others call for cuts in defense spending. Some strongly feel that church should be involved in these issues, while others believe that church must remain detached from any political issues.

The factors contributing to these differences are complex. The ways Christians read and study the Bible are also diverse and even puzzlingly different. There are baffling varieties of spiritualities and worldviews among Christians. Some are flatly contradictory to each other. Black Christian thinkers in the United States and South Africa are seriously questioning whether white racist Christians and black Christians read the same Bible and believe in the same God. How is the church to know which position in these divisive issues is in accord with the Spirit of God? In 1828 the Iroquois leader Red Jacket told a representative of the Boston Missionary Society: "Brother, you say there is but one way to worship and serve the Great Spirit. If there is but one religion, why do you white people differ so much about it?" (*Native American Testimony*, ed. Peter Nabokov, p. 58).

"The Spirit gives us courage to unmask idolatries in church and culture," according to the Presbyterian statement quoted earlier. Are idolatries in church responsible for this confusion? What are idolatries in church? Is it possible for the church to be invaded by idolatries? Is not the church protected by its Lord? Christians differ on this point also.

The Spirit of God does not say directly that "women should be ordained" or "use more tax money on public transportation than on private cars and highways" or "do not smoke" or "do not waste your time with television" or "give this or that applicant a scholarship grant". The Spirit does not give us direct answers. When the congregation engages in honest and thoughtful discussion, the Spirit will help it move forward on its specific problems.

"Let the same mind be in you that was in Christ Jesus" (Phil. 2:5). This "mind" of the congregation is not a uniform or domineering or colonizing or paternalistic or imperialistic or totalitarian mind. It is the mind that follows the "self-emptying" mind of Christ (Phil. 2:5-11). Still, however, it is possible that on some specific issues Christians may have different convictions. Then it is important that a congregation continue in prayer to reflect and work together (Matt. 18:20).

3. The Spirit seems to be saying to us: intersect your stories with the biblical story

A serious self-examining question comes to Christ's congregations: do your Sunday liturgies faithfully and meaningfully present the original sacred story of the Christian faith? Is the sacred story creating hope and life among people? Has the sacred story lost its spiritual appeal and fascination among human souls today? Does the world today demand a new expression of the sacred story?

Has the expression of the sacred story in the liturgy of eucharist ceased to speak meaningfully to the people, and even to the congregation?

When the celebrant says, "All glory be to thee, Almighty God, our heavenly Father, for that thou, of thy tender mercy, didst give thine only Son Jesus Christ to suffer death upon the cross for our redemption", do these solemn words shake the souls of the European people? Is the distance growing between the eucharistic words and everyday human words?

New York City spends US$500 million a year to run shelters for homeless people. On average the city spends $36,000 a year to shelter one family. The programme is plagued by bureaucratic mazes, mismanagement, waste, exploitation and corruption. Homeless people, steadily increasing in number, feel dehumanized in shelters. How do we intersect the story of these homeless with the solemn words of the eucharist of the homeless Christ? Words which do not intersect are empty words.

Do the words of James Baldwin in *Nobody Knows My Name* speak more significantly than the words of the eucharist?

> It is a terrible, an inexorable law that one cannot deny the humanity of another without diminishing one's own: in the face of one's victim, one sees oneself. Walk through the streets of Harlem and see what we, this nation, have become.

The church can exist without the words of Baldwin, but it cannot survive without the words of the eucharist. What Baldwin is saying is a Harlem exegesis of the words of the eucharist. Yet congregations anywhere will find Baldwin helpful to bring the Christian sacred story near to them and their people. The Spirit must be speaking through Baldwin.

The words of Martin Luther King Jr in his famous "Letter from the Birmingham Jail" resound similarly: "Any law that uplifts human personality is just. Any law that degrades human personality is unjust." Here too there is a powerful intersection between the universality of judgment and the particularity of the experience of the oppressed people. This prepares the hearts of the people for the sacred story. Does it not explore and enrich the meaning of the eucharist? Both Baldwin and King re-enacted the sacred story in the 20th century.

Speaking for the African people, Steve Biko once wrote, "We do not believe that God can create people only to punish them eternally after a short period on earth." This expresses Biko's strong stand against missionary theology as he perceived it. One must not believe in God from the fear of hell. Such preaching degrades human personality. Biko's "controversial" words bring the sacred story near to us. The sacred story must intersect with our broken human stories.

There must be a Baldwin, a King and a Biko in Europe. You know them. They are "knocked about", "knocked down" but "never knocked out". The Spirit is near to them and they are near to the Spirit. They make the sacred story powerfully relevant through their own "unsettled" lives. Study their lives. From their own committed lives spring the criteria. They do not look at the problems objectively from a distance and apply a set of criteria. They internalize the criteria. Hence, they risk their lives. There are not two separate entities — Christian congregation and Christian criteria. The Christian congregation, in its life of commitment to Christ, constantly creates the fresh criteria for the discernment of the true Spirit.

Baldwin, King and Biko did not wait for the "deciding moment" (*kairos*) to come. They live with the *kairos*. For them, today is "the day of the Lord" (Amos 5:18f.). They speak for the oppressed people. They represent the people on the periphery. The homeless Jesus is the centre person who affirmed his centrality by going to the periphery. This act of Christ is an important Christian criterion of the truth. The Christian truth does not simply stay at the centre. That would be imperial truth. "This is Jesus, the King of the Jews" (Matt. 27:37) was posted over his head when he was crucified. He was the king when he was the most pushed to the periphery. This is the very message and structure of the gospel itself. Every criterion for the true voice of the Spirit must carry this evangelical quality.

Finally, we have the words of Jesus: "If you greet only your brothers and sisters, what more are you doing than others?" (Matt. 5:47). Jesus comes and greets everyone. As the head of *cosmos* and *ecclesia* Christ upholds the dignity of all people. Christ cannot be confined to a small friendly circle. He is always encountering. For Jesus Christ, and therefore for the holy triune God, no human is a stranger. Therefore, the congregation is exhorted to "extend hospitality to strangers" (Rom. 12:13).

Are our congregational liturgies guided by the Spirit that extends hospitality to strangers? Or are the liturgies only for those who are familiar with them? Is there a "brokenness" ("This is my body, which is broken for you") in our liturgy which invites the stories and symbols of the strangers to come in? Or are they watertight and fixed forever?

Why this focus on liturgy? It is because every day of our life is a liturgy lived before God. The Christian liturgy on Sunday mornings will become less meaningful if it is not stimulated and enriched by encounters with people who are different from us. Christ himself became a stranger (Matt. 25:35). In the gospel of Christ, the stranger plays a crucially important role. The encounters with the stranger remind us of the ever-expanding and inclusive nature of the gospel.

13. And Then What?

Anders Roos

A group in our congregation met now and again to discuss how things ought to be. We had heard of, read about and even seen quite a number of good examples of how life in a congregation could be; and we had plenty of ideas of our own. We longed for a different and more vivid congregational life, but we did not know how to realize our visions — and so they remained as dreams and often as disappointments.

One day we came into contact with someone experienced in development work in contexts other than congregations. That encounter helped us to realize that what was involved was something other than sitting in a group dreaming. There was real work to be done — not work that lasted one or two evenings, or a week, or a month or even a year. If we really wanted change, it would mean hard work during a period as long as five to ten years. Then, perhaps, the result would show up. Were we prepared for such an effort?

Together we discussed Jesus' words in Luke 14:28-32 and their meaning in our situation:

> For which of you, intending to build a tower, does not first sit down and estimate the cost, to see whether he has enough to complete it? Otherwise, when he has laid a foundation and is not able to finish, all who see it will begin to ridicule him, saying, "This fellow began to build and was not able to finish." Or what king, going out to wage war against another king, will not sit down first and consider whether he is able with ten thousand to oppose the one who comes against him with twenty thousand? If he cannot, then, while the other is still far away, he sends a delegation and asks for the terms of peace.

One element of counting the cost could be learning more about the world and society around us and about ourselves. What does our society look like? What people are living there and from where do they come? What do they do at work and in their leisure time? How many are there in

Anders Roos, co-moderator of the European Coordination Group for the ecumenical process of missionary renewal of local congregations, is senior pastor in Sollentuna, the largest parish in the Church of Sweden.

the different age groups? What are their family circumstances? Which companies, factories and other working places are there? What are the schools like? How many pupils and teachers are there? Are there immigrants in the classes? Language problems? Different religions?

Which persons in the various offices, unions and associations and among local authorities are good contacts? How do they value contacts with the church and our congregation? What have the different political parties said about various issues? What do they say about development in our part of town? Are there plans for new buildings, new businesses, for reductions or other changes in activities? How will all this affect people living here?

The questions are many, and we soon realized that we could not manage on our own. We needed help from others if we wanted to go on. It was necessary to distribute the various tasks and to see our own role more in terms of coordinating and inspiring. At the same time, we came to feel that this could be interesting as well as instructive, and so we dared to ask other people — and they were as interested as we were. Together we came to know more about the world we share.

One reason for remaining at the stage of dreams and visions had been that we did not in fact know how much or how little we were able to do or were prepared to do. So we asked what resources we had — how much money, personnel, localities, volunteers, time for new tasks. Was the ongoing work so important that it all had to continue, or could something in the schedule be dropped?

For us this was a new way of thinking and planning. Sometimes we were hesitant. Was all this necessary? Was it perhaps turning into too much administration and planning and too little spirituality? Should the Holy Spirit not guide us in our work like a blowing wind and refreshing breeze? What is the will of God? Gradually we realized that there were three dimensions to work on in congregational life and in our personal lives: depth, participation and outreach. It was also clear that we had to work purposefully according to a plan trying to inspire more and more people to take part in the work.

Depth

The most important question was in fact not what we were doing or how it was done, but *why* we are a Christian congregation right now in this very place. What does God want? What plans does God have for us and for society? To address these questions we gathered for participatory Bible talks — not lectures and sermons by learned theologians but conversations that brought us deeper into God's world and closer to God. This was not easy, but at the same time the Bible started living among us. Every answer raised at least two more questions, and we were forced deeper and deeper into our studies. As the longing for a deeper congregational life grew, we demanded more and more from the priests, and they in turn grew in their ministry. We also came to see clearly that the different congregations and churches could not be allowed to compete with each other. Ecumenical work and the struggle for a deeper and more honest movement towards unity grew slowly but stubbornly.

Through all this our personal spiritual life deepened, and we began to ask ourselves whether our dreams had remained dreams because we had not begun by seeking to trace God's will. Is it at all possible to talk of developing a Christian congregational life without starting in our own spiritual life? The thirst for the living God is motivating power par excellence in every attempt to develop congregational life. The desire of living in God and earnestly looking for God's will is vital for the Christian congregation.

Participation

So far, the work in the congregation had been done by a few people. The services were prepared and led by the priests. The elderly and sick were visited by the deaconess. The youth workers were thought to be the only ones who really understood what young people were thinking and doing. Financial specialists handled the money, administration and organization. In short, most of the work was done by employees, and the people in the congregation were largely viewers and consumers. Least of all was ours a church by and for ordinary people. Only a few were in power and above all was not God but the priest.

We tried to imagine what it would be like if more people took part in the work in the congregation — leading Bible talks, working with children and young people, planning and strategizing, taking part in the practical work to be done, working *together*. Of course, this would sometimes be difficult. It would mean that many opinions and intentions would be forced to melt together and that the result might not be exactly according to one's own wish. But perhaps it would turn out to be better.

And what about all the other organizations and groups struggling for justice, for peace, for preserving the creation, for a more human society, for restored human values, for the rights of refugees? What relations and contacts do we have with them? Do they not bear witness to God's loving will in this world? How can we work together with them to make God more clearly visible in this world? Do we dare to believe that there are signs and evidences of God also outside the churches and outside the congregations — and that those signs and evidences are sometimes even stronger than within the churches?

We realized that God becomes clear in many ways and that it is a task for the congregation to co-ordinate and to let people of good will understand that they are in the service of God. It is also a task for the congregation to use the commitment of different people, to deepen it and to put it in a framework. It is also a task to create situations in which one can grow and mature as a Christian, situations in which it is possible for persons of different backgrounds and convictions to participate and to contribute according to their own abilities.

Outreach

The further we went in our work, the better we understood that God is sending us out into a world that is more and more torn apart every day. Jesus' words in the synagogue in Nazareth also apply to our time: "The Spirit of the Lord is upon me, because he has anointed me to bring good news to the poor. He has sent me to proclaim release to the captives and recovery of sight to the blind, to let the oppressed go free, to proclaim the year of the Lord's favour" (Luke 4:18-19). God sent Jesus Christ into the world at a certain time to make visible and to restore the kingdom of God among the people living then. We are sent to continue that task. It could be said that our task as a Christian congregation is to continue the incarnation, to promote it and bring the kingdom of God closer to its fulfillment.

Planning the work

It became important to start planning the work. We made a schedule for the first part of it. It was a schedule we wanted to keep to, but soon the need for changes showed up. Still, at least we knew in what direction we wanted to move, and we had a framework. Our first attempt to schedule looked like this:

Month 1: The board of the congregation decides on a concentration on the development of congregational life.

Month 2: The planning group gathers, collects material, makes plans for gatherings, seminars, days for inspiration, etc. An analysis of the society around us starts.

Month 5: A large luncheon gathering following the Sunday service on the theme "This is our congregation — but we want more people to come". On participation.

Month 6: A second congregational gathering on the theme "Longing for a deepening of our congregational life". How to reach further into God's world.

Month 7: A third gathering on "The future of our congregation". What tasks is God sending us into?

Month 8: The planning group makes a summary of the work thus far.

Month 10: A fourth gathering on "The congregation participating in the life of the society".

Month 11: A fifth gathering on "Our role in ecumenical life in our local context, our country and around the world".

Month 12: A sixth gathering on "What should we do in our worship services so that more people want to come?"

Month 14: A seventh gathering on "Inviting new groups to co-operate".

Month 16: Several new ideas have now come. We make a summary and make suggestions for the work to be continued.

* * *

And the result? The answer is simply: We do not know! We are still on the move. We have started to make some kind of audit, started to consider more about what God wants us to do. Congregational life according to God's will is demanding and difficult. We do realize that God has a task for us, that the society around challenges us and that we want to be something else than we now are. Where those things meet and are overlaid, a sparkle of the Holy Spirit will be seen. And then...?

Letter to Congregations

"Hear What the Spirit Says to the Churches"

All-European Ecumenical Gathering of Congregational Groups

Grace to you and peace from God, our Father, and our Lord, Jesus Christ.

Europe is changing radically. The mighty have been brought down from their thrones. Oppressed nations have been liberated. Many people have set out for new shores.

But destructive forces are threatening these new beginnings — demonic powers of hatred and violence against strangers, acquisitiveness and self-interest. Many are being forced into poverty while others have become rich or are enriching themselves.

Spiritually, Europe is also changing. Today God gives us the experience of both crisis and grace. Many people have a sense of spiritual emptiness. At the same time, God is giving a new spiritual start in other countries, like rain after a long drought. Congregations are faced with a wealth of new tasks and opportunities. The harvest is great.

As representatives of congregations all over Europe, we at this meeting in Potsdam have shared joys and uncertainties, strengths and weaknesses in this changing situation. The call and the strength of the Spirit to renew our congregations, which we have received in this exchange, is what we should like to pass on to you.

We were surprised how different we were. In our opening worship God's word rang out in 27 different languages. All these different languages represent just as many differences of history and culture. And we are also different as churches or even divided by our different confessions. Is it possible for us to understand one another despite these differences? Is it possible to learn from one another despite these differences? We have experienced that it is possible.

Our common desire for renewal binds us together. Our common prayer for guidance by God's Spirit opens us up to one another.

"Hear what the Spirit says to the churches."

Hearing begins with conversion, with spiritual purification. Prayer and patience are the conditions for listening properly. We have tried to listen together to what the Spirit wants to say to us, the churches in Europe. The Spirit of God is a Spirit of love. He leads us to the weak. Today in Europe the weak comprise refugees and the unemployed, the lonely and the lost. What is the Spirit trying to say to the churches through them? The Spirit of God is a Spirit of community. He directs us to overcome the barriers that separate people from one another.

At this meeting in Potsdam we have told one another about our congregations — how we have been trying back home to listen to the voice of the Spirit. We are grateful for the many encouraging examples of new beginnings and renewal. Now we know we are not alone. We belong to a family that goes beyond our borders. We are members of the one body of Christ. So we want to have more contacts with congregations in other countries. "If one member suffers, all suffer together with it; if one member is honoured, all rejoice together with it" (1 Cor. 12:26).

This applies to the worldwide family of the church and to our congregation locally. That is the place where everyone can experience that it is true: God loves me. I am important. The Spirit has given me a gift as well. And the community needs my gift.

We feel that what we can do to pass on God's love is very small. But the little that we can do is important. God makes the little things that we do in the strength of his Spirit into big ones. He makes them part of his plan — his plan to save the world.

"My grace is sufficient for you, for power is made perfect in weakness" (2 Cor. 12:9), says the Lord.

Potsdam, Germany
19-25 July 1993